I0621184

WITH WORDS WE WEAVE

Texas High Plains Writers

2019 Anthology

Cover design by Mike Akins

Cover Photo by Jonathan Baker

Book layout by Ryan McSwain

ISBN: 978-1-7338621-0-3

First Edition: 2019

www.texashighplainswriters.com

CONTENTS

INTRODUCTION

KR Brorman

"There's a vastness here and I believe that the people breathe that vastness into their soul. They dream big dreams and think big thoughts, because there is nothing to hem them in." - Conrad Hilton

The best way to discover a culture is to listen to the stories. Cultural riches spring from the Texas High Plains—majestic skies at dawn and dusk, towering storms that sweep the fertile soil, people of heroic deeds and quiet dignity—and we the storytellers are the guardians of these vast treasures.

In this anthology, you will find cowboys and soldiers; husbands, wives, and children; horses, bears, pigs (guinea and oink); fear, faith, and love—stories as varied and vast as the people and country that inspired them.

This collection of short stories, inspirational essays, and poetry is truly a labor of love. Member writers and artists from across the plains contributed humor, heartache, and truth to these pages. You will discover works from best-selling authors and first-timers nested together.

For nearly one hundred years, Texas High Plains Writers has supported and encouraged writers with an eye to a hundred more years. Founded by Laura V. Hamner in 1920 as Panhandle Pen Women, the organization has matured and changed with the times, becoming Panhandle Professional Writers in 1987 to reflect the growing membership of men in our ranks, and becoming Texas High Plains Writers in 2015 to broaden our appeal to beginning as well as professional writers.

Writers of all ages and interests will find camaraderie and benefit from the collaborative spirit in Texas High Plains Writers. The critique groups and guest speakers foster creative courage and help writers at every level perfect their craft and navigate the ever-changing world of publication. Membership is open to anyone, published or not, with a love of or desire to learn about the art of the written word.

Texas High Plains Writers is excited to offer this latest compilation. Previous anthologies may be found in Amarillo's Downtown Library. Everyone has a story to tell; we hope these inspire you to tell yours and join us for the 2020 Centennial edition.

Texas High Plains Writers
texashighplainswriters.com

To Grandpa

Saving You in Your Granddaughter's Eyes

Mevanee Parmer

My young eyes, watching you there, stooping alone, at the end of a
red row
Of warm, sandy loam so expertly plowed
It looks like art.
Your thin, old body bends down effortlessly
As you lovingly sift, then sniff the crumbly scarlet soil between your
fingers.
Near Quitaque Creek, this rich dirt with the right measure of rain,
And some good labor, grows cotton, corn, maize
And feeds family through decades. And it belongs to you:
The strength, the time, this sandy farm. Soil packed
Under your boots and fingernails, the proof,
And on windy days under your collar and eyelids.

I keep long vigil for you, coming in to lunch,
From the far field, trudging the tractor's hot sandy path.
We three sit at the red-gingham-oilcloth-covered table, steaming
Hot with fresh peas, beans, corn and greens, cool tomatoes, picked
this morning.

The taste of warm sunshine heats our mouths, spreading across our
smiling faces.
My quiet grandma cooked her crops patiently in many pots,
And served up the fresh-fried chicken which was an hour ago
Skipping headless around the yard. You say you will take me
On the tractor, though Grandma disapproves. Fresh outdoors,
Riding through the fields, my joy almost ends in disaster:
As I toppled backwards toward dust and plow, you
Pulled me back to safety, your hand firmly grasping my thin arm.
Then you stopped the tractor, grabbing me to your beating heart.
It is the last day you let me share the pleasure
Of ploughing the fields with you.

I come to you, still strong beyond your years, striding
Across the pasture, stirring your own dust cloud
In your heavy brown boots and blue overalls,
Plucking the milkweed as you go, leading the cows in,
Clucking to urge them home, and as though to old friends,
Calling their names as the sun sets a glory
In the clouds. You call to my young self who has wandered
To join you in this twilight walk. Later we will be
Awakened by thunder, and wrapped in blankets run
To the little gray cinder-block house, sunbaked and holding the day's
heat,
Then cooling as the rain pours down. While tiny chicks chirp
Beneath the bed springs, we huddle, calm and safe,
As gray-green clouds churn above us.

I stand quietly as you kneel, still in love with the soil, then walking
In careful strides with me through your loved, heavily-spiced
Pear orchard, avoiding the ripe fruit covering the ground. For it is fall
And most of the crop has been picked over.
Needy neighbors, birds and bugs have had their bite. But the soft
winds bring
An inviting murmur to attend the fruit harvest.

TO GRANDPA

Sorting, I chance on a smooth green pear with only a faint scent.
But you tell me the brown ones are better, and so they are.
Sweet and crunchy, the succulence spills down my chin.

I wince, embarrassed as you, sitting stalwart,
Sullen in your chair, listen to them plotting,
Your own blood, especially the flame-haired daughters,
To move you, due to their great love, off your land.
Their claim: they didn't want to find you dead in the field,
Planted in the dirt like the crops you loved.
Thus, isolation came to town, to a bare yard,
With the wife of your youth, to a cramped house without the
Adornment of cedars and company of trumpet flowers
And wild red roses you had cultivated in the country.

Far from the cool dipper that hung beside your own well,
And far from the milk cows you brought in nightly.
But you found neighbors' gardens to revive,
Tilling up their turf with your faded gray-blue tractor,
Sifting their soil between the wrinkled skin of your bent fingers,
Still alive in the smell of earth and wind.

I stand soberly aside and observe you once again,
In the stark hospital hall: the doctor says flatly, "Your wife will not
come home."
And when there is no more wife, no more farm, no more strength
To climb upon a tractor, no more orchard to share, no use for the
labor,
No more fields to plant and harvests to reap, no more sheds to build,
You, *imagining yourself alone and without use,* went out
Beside the solitary stand of zinnias you planted,
Their startling neon colors perfect in the stinging summer sun,
Their smell harsh and bitter. You pulled the red metal porch chair
beside them

And reached again to hold the soil you had loved and worked all your life.
Then slowly taking the gun in your trembling hands,
 You returned,
Dust to dust.

Mevanee Parmer learned she was truly a writer when her ninth grade English teacher told her she was. She was the inimitable Mrs. Plachek at Travis Middle School in Amarillo. Mevanee hopes she was right. Mevanee has been writing and teaching writing ever since, from middle school to college level. Having a passion for sharing the voices of her High Plains ancestors, she's writing a biography of her prairie grandmother, as well as poetry. Her husband Phill is also a writer, English teacher, and go-to editor. They live in Amarillo and enjoy travelling to visit their three children and seven delightful grandchildren.

Paper Heart

Linda Broday

Texas 1882
Late Spring

Sunlight glinted off the Rock Creek, Texas sign out Rainey Wilder's window. She took a deep breath and gathered her courage, praying she hadn't come on a fool's errand. The train belched, smoke billowing up in white clouds as the steam engine protested the stop.

She gripped her worn carpetbag in a trembling hand and stood. At the exit, the conductor smiled and tipped his hat. "Have a good day, ma'am."

That would depend on the good Lord and the shape of the house where she was born.

Rainey lifted her frayed hem to avoid muck from someone's shoe and stepped onto the platform. Folks waiting to claim the arrivals rushed forward.

No welcome committee waited for her. No one to claim the weary spinster.

No one with open arms or a kind word.

She kept her gaze lowered, not glancing at her surroundings because it didn't much matter how the buildings appeared. This was her last chance to make a new life, to run from a past that dogged her. She had nowhere left to go.

Make it or fail, here in Rock Creek was where it would happen.

Her heart in her throat, she hurried past the happy reunions and turned down a side street of the town that bore familiarity, yet a strange newness about it also. She'd once been happy here. Carefree.

Maybe something of her old life still existed although her only family rested below ground in the cemetery just beyond the row of houses.

Someone had once told her that people couldn't go home again. She prayed they were wrong because that sliver of hope was all she had to cling to.

Her heart seemed made of fragile paper, ripped by trials and despair, lying discarded in a rain puddle.

Rainey stopped at the corner, under a large elm she'd once climbed as a girl. Dropping her bag, she plopped down in the shade and finally allowed herself a look around. The sight made her stomach clench into a knot. The once beautiful homes were shabby and rundown. No laughing children played. If this is the condition of the best part of the neighborhood, what lay farther down—where she'd lived? She couldn't bear to think about what ifs and maybes. Life was uncertain enough.

When she got to the end of the street, she stared in disbelief, biting her knuckles to stifle a sharp cry. The only true home she'd ever known was a burned-out hulk, the charred beams in stark relief against an ever-darkening sky. A distant peal of thunder rumbled.

Rainey dropped to the ground next to her carpetbag. When the rains came, she moved underneath the porch and curled up, shivering. This wasn't how she pictured life at thirty—alone, unloved, unwanted.

Sometime near midnight, she dozed off. Warm, soft fur pressed against her and a tongue licked her cheek, startling her awake.

By the light of a rustler's moon that came from behind a cloud, she made out a little puppy. She pulled it next to her, petting the soft head until it whined and snuggled into her warmth. Somehow, she didn't feel quite so alone.

At dawn, she crawled from beneath the old porch, clutching the puppy. He glanced up at her expectantly and licked her hand. He was a pretty thing and the placement of black, brown and white on his body put him in the beagle category.

"I'm going to call you Wags." The minute Rainey set him down he spun in a circle and yipped. To her, it suggested that he liked the name. "We're both orphans it seems."

The first order of business—find something to eat. Deciding her carpetbag would be safe in her makeshift bedroom, she strolled toward the grove of trees at the road's end. The puppy, its pink tongue hanging out, scampered along beside her as though happy to have a friend. A short time later, she found some wild plums and strawberries. She devoured all she could hold then stuffed her pockets while Wags chased the birds.

On the return, Wags found a dead squirrel and that served as his breakfast. Rainey knocked on the door of a house and asked to drink from their well. She never took anything without asking.

For two days, they kept the same routine and no one gave them a second glance. On the third morning when she crawled from the porch, an old woman hobbled toward her. "Young lady, you're trespassing."

Rainey's stomach clenched. "I'm not bothering anyone. I used to live here."

The old woman squinted through glasses, her eyes as huge as owls through the thick lenses. "Were you kin to the Wilders?"

"Their daughter, Rainey, ma'am."

"Well, I swear. I haven't seen you in years. Didn't recognize you. I'm Ida Mooney."

The name jogged Rainey's memory and she could see faint, familiar features buried under the layers of saggy wrinkles and heavy jowls. "Nice to see you, Mrs. Mooney."

Wags sniffed around the woman's feet then sat back expectantly on his haunches.

"What are you doing back, Rainey?"

"I returned to Rock Creek and thought I could stay here. No one sent word the placed burned."

Even so, she still would've come since she had no other options.

"Lordy, what a fire!" Mrs. Mooney's jowls quivered like a bowl of jelly. "Flames shot as high as the sky and I feared every house on the street would catch. Have you eaten, girl?"

"No, ma'am."

"Well, what are you waiting for? I'll share what I fixed."

Wags fell into step with them and at the house, Mrs. Mooney held the door for the little beagle. The once spotless house was cluttered and dirty, nothing like Rainey remembered. Deep sadness cast a pall over her as memories swirled of rainy days in Ida's kitchen munching on cookies hot from the oven.

Other times, she'd curled up on a window seat in the parlor, lost in an adventure within the pages of a book swept over her. She'd loved spending time at Ida Mooney's.

What had happened to the proud woman to let the house fall into shambles?

Rainey passed through to the kitchen and soon sat down to the first hot food she and Wags had eaten in days. The dog wolfed down his food then laid in front of the stove to doze.

Ida Mooney buttered a slice of bread. "What happened to you, Rainey dear? I heard you went to live with your sister Lucy. She took sick if I recall."

"Lucy had a bad heart and needed help with her little family. She passed on two months ago." Rainey struggled to find the words. Lucy had been her best friend and to watch her wither away had taken all Rainey's strength. But the shock came a few short weeks later when Lucy's husband remarried and the newlyweds booted Rainey out. Thank goodness she'd saved enough for a train ticket and Rock Creek was the only place she knew.

"I'm very sorry to hear that. Lucy was a sweet girl. Milk, dear?"

"Yes, please." Rainey pushed her empty glass toward the woman. "Now, I suppose I'll look for work. Would you know of anyone hiring?"

"You're looking at her."

"You need someone to help?"

"In more ways than one." Ida ran a trembling hand over her eyes. "Honey, I can barely see, can't walk good, and you probably noticed the condition of this house. I haven't went to collect my mail at the mercantile in a month of Sundays or replenished my pantry. I've gotten old and I'm all alone."

Rainey slid from her chair and knelt beside the old woman. "I'll help you, but I won't take money for it."

She'd do it because that's what you did for a friend.

"I won't hear of that. I'll pay you one way or another. You'll move in here and be my companion. We'll be each other's family, Rainey dear." Ida's gnarled hand smoothed Rainey's hair. "It'll be like my Hannah is alive again."

Family. That's what life was all about—having someone to care about you.

Rainey stood and went to fetch her carpetbag. Her heart was light as she unpacked and then went to work cleaning the house where she'd spend many a pleasurable hour.

That afternoon, she walked to the mercantile for Ida. She collected her mail and bought everything Ida needed. She hummed a song and smiled at everyone she met.

Maybe home could never be exactly like it was before but this one had found her instead of the other way around and it fit like a comfortable pair of old shoes.

On the way back, she stopped where a nice man entertained a group of laughing children and sat on a bench to watch. He glanced her way and smiled, then took out some colorful paper and scissors. Rainey watched as he kept cutting and glancing at her, curious what he was making.

After a few moments he strolled to her and bowed with a flourish, handing her a beautiful, pink paper heart. "A token for a pretty lady. Forgive me. You remind me of my sister."

Rainey's cheeks heated. "Thank you. It's quite lovely."

His eyes twinkled like bright, blue diamonds and the smile deepened the lines of his crow's feet. "Are you new? I haven't seen you before."

"I grew up here and only recently returned." Rainey stood and gathered her purchases.

"Welcome home then. I'll see you around. By the way, I'm Jim Fletcher."

"Rainey Wilder." She couldn't have stopped the grin if she tried.

It's funny that before this day she'd felt as if her heart was made of nothing but paper, torn and soaked. Now the kindness of others had made it whole. Kindness and caring seemed the secret to a life well-lived.

A bird perched on a low limb of a nearby tree, singing to beat all.

Happiness like she hadn't felt in a long time swept through Rainey. Home seemed to have found her instead of the other way around.

She had Ida Mooney and Wags and here was where she belonged.

Linda Broday is a New York Times and USA Today bestselling author of 24 books and novellas and a proud member of Texas High Plains Writers since 2002. In 2018, she was named WRITER OF THE YEAR. Linda loves writing about the cowboy way of life and finds plenty of inspiration at home in the Panhandle.

Amazon Author Page: amazon.com/Linda-Broday/e/B001JRXWB2
Website: LindaBroday.com
Facebook: facebook.com/linda.broday1
Twitter: @LBroday
Goodreads: goodreads.com/author/show/1204489.Linda_Broday

In the Heart of a Ranger

Mary McMinn

Josh Campbell read the wanted poster. The three outlaws were mean enough. They killed the banker and then, as they left town, killed a young boy just for the fun of it. Well, it wouldn't be his problem anymore. As of today, he was no longer a Texas Ranger. He dropped the dodger onto the captain's desk.

Captain McNally stood and offered a handshake. "I'm sure sorry to see you leave us. You've done a fine job."

He shook hands with the Captain. "It's time I took care of my family and the ranch. Ellie lost our last baby from carrying the load herself and I need to be there this time."

"I understand and good luck, Son. If you ever want to come back, you'll always have a place with the Texas Rangers."

"Thank you, Sir. I'm a family man and a homesteader now. Here's my badge."

"Keep it, Son. Someday you'll find out, once a Ranger, always a Ranger."

Josh nodded, slipped the badge into the pocket of his shirt and left the Captain to his work.

Outside, on the boardwalk, Josh met his friend and neighbor, Dick Chambers.

"Hey, you get your man?" Dick pumped his arm like he was pumping for water. He was a big man with a heart as large as his ability to wrestle a steer to the ground when needed. He slapped Josh on the shoulder, nearly knocking him off his feet.

"I got him. Dropped him off at the sheriff's office. Just finished up with the paperwork."

"That's good. Glad you're back."

"Thank your wife for me. It relieved my mind to know she was keeping an eye on Ellie."

"Shoot, no one could have stopped her. Jeannie loves them newborn babies like they was her own."

"You ever had any babies of your own?" Josh asked.

"Nope. Doc doesn't know why. But, Jeannie says it's God's will for her to be helping bring them into the world. If she had any of her own, she might not have the time to take care of all the mothers around here. It pleasures her something fierce to help. When you get home, will you send her back? She went over to your place yesterday morning."

"She spent the night?" Josh asked.

"Not to worry. When she checked on Ellie a couple of days ago, it was a false alarm. You know how first babies are. They like to take their time."

"Except this isn't exactly our first baby."

"Yeah. I'm sorry. I forgot you lost a boy last year when he tried to come into this world too early. But, Jeannie said Ellie is doing real good."

Dick raised his voice to the wind. Josh had already mounted his horse and was heading for home.

Josh tried not to worry. The baby wasn't due yet. Ellie had assured him there was plenty of time for him to take care of his business with the Rangers. The Captain had insisted there was no one else to send. All his other men were busy in Galveston helping with a riot.

Josh had promised his wife he'd be back in time for the baby and, now, if Jennie had spent the night, something must have gone wrong. He'd never forgive himself if she lost this baby, too.

The first one was hard enough. A little boy. He seemed perfect in every way. Just too small. The doctor said he wasn't ready for this world. His little lungs just weren't big enough.

Ellie would never forgive him either. A promise is a promise. She could handle a lot, but not this.

No. That was wrong. She was the most patient and kind-hearted person he'd ever known. She constantly told him how much she loved him. But he didn't know how many babies a woman could stand to lose. The last one had taken its toll on both of them.

Ellie would tell him she loved him, then turn away before he could touch her. It took months before she quit crying herself to sleep.

She'd cry but he couldn't. Until one day the pain was so strong he couldn't help himself. She put her arms around him. Comforting him. And then they cried together, holding each other for the longest time. After that, she'd let him kiss her and hold her.

When she told him she was in a family way again, he couldn't help but notice the fear in her eyes. He promised her he'd be there this time.

Josh reined in to give his horse, Jasper, a breather. Smoke from a campfire rose just to the south of them. A camp so close to town was unusual for this time of day. If it had been getting late the night before and they stopped, they would have already headed for town.

Someone might be in trouble. Or worse. They might be up to no good, maybe planning an attack on the town. Well, he couldn't find out anything just sitting there.

The lawman in him reminded him to approach with caution. Three men lingered around the fire, watching a Navajo woman cook. Something about the scene gave Josh the willies, then he noticed. The woman was hobbled like a horse. She could move around the campfire, but could never outrun the men if she had wanted to get away from them.

The men resembled the outlaws on the poster in the captain's office. They probably stopped here to wait for dark before going into town to do whatever they planned.

Josh took a deep breath, a moment of indecision entering his soul. His wife needed him. He wanted to pass on by and pretend he hadn't seen them, but the Ranger in him wouldn't allow it. The hobbled woman was in trouble. The town might be, too.

He moved as close as he dared, keeping the sun behind him. A large knife jutted from the ground, probably where the woman stuck it while she cooked. If only she could read his thoughts, maybe she could get hold of it and protect herself when he made his move.

Cold bumps rose on his neck. He raised his eyes to the woman and realized she was staring at him. Their eyes met. Her eyes dropped to the knife and then back to him. He nodded. She winked and returned to her cooking, shifting her position closer to the knife. She was Navajo. She understood and was ready. Josh had no doubt she knew how to use the knife. Probably would have already if the ropes hadn't hobbled her and there hadn't been three of them to fend off.

"Hello to camp," Josh hollered as he stepped out of the shrub he'd been hiding in.

All three men pulled their guns. The woman grabbed the knife and swiftly plunged it into the chest of the man closest to her. She rolled to the ground as bullets flew into the afternoon. After the smoke settled, only the woman and Josh were still alive.

"Are you okay?" Josh asked the woman.

"I am okay." Her words were choppy.

Josh checked the three outlaws and pulled the knife from the one the woman had killed. He cut away the ropes that kept her hobbled.

"You speak good English."

"Yes. I was taught the white man's tongue. I worked for the woman of a general in your army."

"How did you end up with these outlaws?"

"One day, my tribe raided the house and took me back to live with them. I helped the old chief talk with the white men. The other squaws not like me. The chief thought me special. They tell him me too much trouble. I was traded for a horse. It was a good horse."

"No doubt. You think you could take these men to town and explain to Captain McNally?"

"Would he believe the words of a Chiricahua woman?"

He sighed. "I better go with you."

The captain had been right. Once a lawman, always a lawman. He just hoped Ellie would understand.

He kept telling himself she was okay. She wasn't alone. Jennie was with her. But, he had promised. Over the years, he had broken so many promises because of his job. And, now, after quitting the Rangers, here he was, letting her down again, because of the job.

It only took a little while to get the three men laid across their saddles and head toward town. An hour later, He was heading home again.

Clouds had gathered and rain splattered the yellow slicker Josh wore. He had to get to the crossing before the rain got heavier and the creek swelled into a torrent. He'd be forced to take the long way around and that would add another hour to the trip home. And he had to get home before it was too late!

If only he hadn't run into those outlaws. He would have already been home. He could have taken the Apache with him, checked on Ellie and then taken the outlaws into town. It didn't matter now. What was done was done.

The creek wasn't bad yet, but another twenty minutes would have cost the extra time. Josh let Jasper get a quick drink and then nudged him to cross over. They took their time. Anything could be floating in the moving water. One misstep and they'd both be goners.

An hour later, the rain had stopped. Josh drew rein and leaned on the saddle horn. Jasper dipped his head and nibbled on a sprig of grass. He was as tired as his rider. A soft breeze blew up. The mount's ears pricked forward, his nostrils flared. He dipped his head and snorted.

"You smell it, too, don't you boy?" Josh rubbed Jasper's neck. With a nudge of his knee, the mount sprung forward. Josh gave the Strawberry Roan his head and the trot turned into a run. Home! Just over the hill.

With bated breath, Josh opened the door to the two-room shack he and Ellie called home, ready for whatever greeted him.

Ellie stood there, beside the dry basin, her face in shadow. "I missed you," she whispered.

He closed the distance. Her hands cupped the back of his head and their lips met. The kiss was short and they cradled each other. He patted her belly where a baby once dwelled. He dreaded to hear the words.

"I missed you, too," he said. I'm sorry I wasn't here."

"It's okay. Jeannie just left. She wanted to get home before the rains got worse."

Was she avoiding the words that needed said? To tell him they had lost another child. Guilt flooded his soul and tears filled his eyes. "I should have refused the Captain. You shouldn't have been left alone."

"Come with me." She pulled him toward the alcove where their bed stood, the empty cradle nearby.

She sat on the side of the bed and patted the place beside her. "Come, sit here." She turned behind her and lifted a bundle of blanket. "I wasn't alone. Your daughter would like to meet you."

"A girl?"

"Yes, my darling." Laughter hinted in her voice. "I'm sorry she wasn't a boy. I know how bad you wanted a son."

"A son?" He stared at the bundle in his arms. The baby whimpered. He looked from the baby to his wife. The smile on her face filled him with joy.

He shook sense into his head. "No, darling. It never mattered to me."

"But a man always wants a son, an heir."

"I just want my family to be healthy and happy. We will be happy, won't we?"

"Oh, yes, my darling. I do love you. And, I always will."

Josh began to cry. His energy exhausted.

She pulled him close. They held each other and admired the wonder of a new life.

Now came the hard part. To tell her that he couldn't quit his job. But somehow, he knew she'd understand.

Once a Ranger, always a Ranger.

HARRIET,

THE LONELY PIG

Audrey Cannady Massingill

Dear Cousin Carol,

I'm sorry it has taken me so long to answer your last letter, but we have been busy getting settled out here in Colorado. It has been three months since we brought the mobile home out to this lovely spot and I must admit I am really enjoying my first taste of country living.

The land we bought nestles at the foot of Mesa Verde National Park and our home site is filled with trees. We have only two other families sharing the dirt road; the Hennemans, who are about a mile up from us, and Jack and Nellie Allum, about fifty yards down. There are so many trees between us and the Allum's trailer, however; that they seem much further away. We have a feeling of quiet isolation but actually we are only a half mile from our mail box at the highway. In all four directions, the views are splendid. From the bedroom window we have a grand view of the San Juan Mountains. From the kitchen, we look out at Mesa Verde Park. And everywhere there are wild flowers and towering trees.

Debbie is making the transition from city to country life more easily than I had anticipated. She was apprehensive about starting high school in Mancos, but when she learned that there were eleven boys and only three girls in her freshman class, she perked up. Since one of those eleven boys is "Handsome Hunk Greg," her enthusiasm for school is remarkable.

Hans, the lion-hearted dachshund, is keeping busy exploring his new surroundings. He has already had one bout with a porcupine, but the experience hasn't dimmed his fighting spirit one bit. You know him, he'll throw his fifteen-pound dog body up against anything.

Jim, of course, is right in his element. Living in the country brings back boyhood memories of his family's farm near Polar. The problem is every time he goes strolling down memory lane, he feels he must drag Debbie and me kicking and screaming along with him. And the simplest things set him off.

Take, for instance, an innocent remark I made several weeks ago. "Honey, how about pork chops for supper tonight?" This led to a story of how his family used to butcher hogs in the fall. He became downright eloquent in describing how his mother loved to make lard in a big kettle over an outdoor fire, and of the delicious sausages she made. Somehow, before I fully realized what was happening, it was decided that we would butcher our own hog.

The next evening we all piled into the truck and went to Breen to the Harris's pig farm. While Mr. Harris showed Jim several hundred identical-looking large hogs, Mrs. Harris showed Debbie and me the nursery which held several hundred identical-looking piglets. There was also another building with several hundred identical-looking medium pigs. After a while it seemed to me as if all the pigs in the entire world were gathered at this one farm. After Jim made his choice, the men loaded our pig into the horse trailer for the trip back to the house.

When we got home, we put the pig into the pen outside our bedroom window. Debbie and I decided to name the pig Harry. When Jim told us that the pig wasn't Harry material, we changed its name to Harriet.

The next day, as a special treat for Harriet, we went down to Nunn's apple orchard and picked up a bunch of windfall apples. We all had a great day watching her eat them. The only problem was Hans. He was jealous of our new pet and every time we let him out of the house, he would go to the pen and bark at Harriet.

All in all, things were going much more smoothly than Jim's projects usually do. I know, Carol, I should have known better.

The next day, Monday, we left for work and school. Late that afternoon, Debbie called me. "Mother, Harriet is not in her pen!" I replied with my standard answer to all problems: "Debbie, call your father and tell him."

With visions of pork chops scattered on the highway, I hurried home. Jim arrived about the same time I did and organized us into a search party. We finally spotted Harriet casually strolling in the field beyond the house. She looked a lot bigger outside of the pen.

Jim began herding Harriet back to the yard and Debbie and I were supposed to walk on each side of her to keep her going in the right direction. However, faced with a 250-pound hog, we mainly kept out of her way. In spite of us, Jim eventually got Harriet back to the yard. But every time he tried to put her into the pen, Hans began barking and off she would go. Finally, Jim put Hans down in the root cellar where Harriet couldn't hear him bark. He then armed Debbie and me with big sticks, positioned us strategically around the pen, and said, "If either of you yelps and jumps back when that pig gets close to you, I'm going to shove you in the root cellar with Hans when this is over."

With these inspiring words echoing in our ears, sticks in hand, we vowed to stand firm against the enormous beast. Luckily our resolve wasn't tested because at that moment, Harriet calmly walked into the pen and began munching apples.

The next day I went home for lunch and was greeted by the sight of Harriet standing in the front yard casually looking around. Dashing into the house, I called Jim and screeched into the phone, "Harriet is out again! Do something!" He came home and we had another pig roundup. After the fun was over, while eating lunch and speculating how that pig could be getting out of the pen, we looked out just in time to see her climb over the top of the fence and stroll away.

That evening we had a family meeting. After much discussion, we finally realized that the reason Harriet broke out was not a thirst for freedom but a quest for companionship. After all, she was used to the company of all those other pigs. She was lonely. The only solution would be to keep her company until we could butcher her later in the week. We decided that Debbie would stay home from school the next day and pig sit. She was not happy. "But if I don't go to school, I won't see Greg." With sincere sympathy, Jim answered, "That's too bad. We can't afford to lose that hog." With a final heart rending cry—"I will be the only girl in Mancos who doesn't talk to Greg tomorrow!"—Debbie stomped to her room.

The next morning, a more cheerful Debbie took a lawn chair, the portable radio, and lots of snacks to the yard. Harriet, delighted with the constant company, stayed peacefully in the pen. The two of them had a good day munching away together. Hans, in an excess of jealousy, barked all day.

The next day it was my turn to stay home with Harriet, so Debbie could go to school to see the Handsome Hunk. I took a lawn chair, the portable radio, lots of snacks, and, of course, a book to the yard. Harriet and I had a good morning munching away together. Hans, resigning himself to another pet in the family, tried to make friends, but Harriet just ignored him and kept on eating. To express his feelings of rejection, Hans barked all morning.

After lunch, I went to work and Jim took over. By the time Debbie and I returned in the evening, the pen was empty. All weekend Jim tried to teach me how to make lard and sausages and other goodies, but, to be honest, I didn't love this activity like his mother had. And I don't think Debbie and I will ever have the heart to actually eat any of it.

I will close for now as I need to start fixing supper. I wonder if Jim would like roast beef tonight?

Love and Laughter,
Your New-to-the-Country Cousin, Audrey

Audrey Cannady Massingill is a transplanted Texan. She has been doing genealogy for the past thirty years and began writing to get her family stories in shape in order to share them with relatives and friends. Besides genealogy, she is writing her memoirs. She also writes humorous stories about her dogs, which may or may not be true. She has published several genealogy books and a few small books of her memoirs and family stories.

The Night We Ran Jim

Richard Brown

There wasn't much to do in McKinney, Texas in 1931. They say necessity is the mother of invention and that's where this story starts, with the game we teenage boys invented to liven up those long, hot, dog days of summer.

I first met Jim White on a Tuesday in June. He was sitting at the soda fountain in the pharmacy. I approached him and stuck out my hand. "Jack Griffin." Happy to meet someone, Jim introduced himself and we began to talk. He was staying the summer with his aunt, Agnes Smith, the lady who lived in the big two story at the end of Third Street.

Like all the summer transplants, he was hoping to meet kids his age. I took him under my wing, so to speak, telling him about our little town. After we had talked a bit, I figured Jim was primed and ready to hear the magic words: "Hey Jim, You like girls?"

"Sure, I like girls," he answered, a hint of excitement creeping into his voice.

"That's exactly what I hoped you'd say. My girl is Alice Taylor. Her younger sister, Mary Lou, has been wanting to double date with us but she hasn't got a guy of her own. So, double this Saturday night?"

"Maybe. I mean, what's she like?" He squirmed a bit from surprise.

"She's perfect. That's what she's like. If I weren't datin' Alice, I'd be after Mary Lou in a heartbeat."

"If she's so perfect, why don't she already have a guy?"

"She just turned sixteen last month. She weren't allowed to date before that. And she did have a fellow after her, Larry Thomas, but he moved away two months ago. Broke her heart, him leaving just before she's allowed to date. So, there you are, sweet sixteen and never been kissed."

"Well, then, sure," Jim agreed, looking satisfied.

"Great! Alice will set it up with Mary Lou. All you got to do is be ready on Saturday. You got some nice clothes don't you?"

"Nothin special."

I ended up taking Jim down to the mercantile. He ponied up most of his summer savings (it was 1931 after all) on a new shirt. As we shopped, I dribbled out more details about Mary Lou. How pretty she was, her long brown hair, and gentle nature. He went home about as warmed up as a guy could get for a date with a perfect stranger.

The next day I told my best friend, Joe Boy Barnett, about the new guy. Joe made sure to meet up with Jim at the soda fountain and confirm everything I said about Mary Lou. He got Jim even more excited, if such a thing were possible. Plus, Joe owned a shotgun. That would come in handy for Joe's part come Saturday.

And, of course, I spoke with Mr. Taylor. Mr. Taylor was our history teacher at the high school. He loved his students almost as much as his students loved him. He promised to be ready when the time came.

Saturday evening rolled around and I borrowed my mom's spiffy new Model A. Feeling all fancy, I drove over to Third Street to pick up Jim. He stepped out the door pressed and polished. Sure enough, he was going all out to put his best foot forward. I admired his effort. He looked and smelled perfect for a night out with a pretty girl.

We left Jim's place right after sunset. I explained to Jim that the farm where the girls lived was about five miles out. I drove around on dirt covered country roads for half an hour. Once it was good and dark, and Jim was hopelessly lost, I started in telling him the terrible truth about Taylor.

"Listen, Jim. When we get there, you let me do the talking. Last time I was there, Old Man Taylor told me never to come back. He's a mean sonofabitch. But I don't give a damn what he says, we're taking those girls to the dance. You're with me, right?"

This, of course, was big news to Jim. The whole week he'd been told nothing but rainbows and roses about his date. All of a sudden, here comes an unexpected twist, a dark turn of events, so to speak. He spins around in his seat and asks me, "Why didn't you mention this before now?"

"I've tangled with Taylor before and nothin's come of it. He makes a lot of threats, but just stand your ground when we get there and we'll handle that crusty old bastard just fine."

Jim's face scrunched up as he digested my answer. When I figured he was as anxious as I could make him, I turned down the road to the Taylor place. By this time it was pitch black out. I pulled up in front of the farm house, honked that ah-ooo-gah horn a few times and told Jim, "Come on, let's go get the girls."

Jim got out of the car, but he didn't seem particularly anxious to race me to the porch. This told me he was properly primed for what was about to happen. And what was about to happen did happen. Mr. Taylor came bustin' out the screen door, the lone light bulb dangling from the living room ceiling illuminating the room behind him and casting a shadow in our direction.

"What the hell you doing here?" He yelled. "I done told you, Jack Griffin, you ain't welcome here. Get the hell off my property." Mr. Taylor dressed the part too. He wore an old pair of overalls with no shirt underneath. He looked every bit the country bumpkin he was pretending to be.

"You don't tell me what to do, Taylor. Alice is my girl and I'm here to take her to the dance. Jim, here, is taking Mary Lou. The girls are coming with us so you just stay the hell outta the way."

"You can't talk to me like that, you lousy good-for-nothing heathen," Taylor shouted. He proceeded to lay into me with insults. Before he finished I started back in on him, each of us yelling to beat the band.

Jim shrank away from the porch even as I edged closer. Finally, Taylor and I were an arm's length apart. This was the moment of truth. Taylor opened the screen door, reached back inside and brought out a shotgun.

That was my cue. I yelled as loud as I was able, "He's got a gun! Run, Jim, run!" And Jim, to his ever-loving credit, ran. Lordy, lordy, how he ran. I have no idea if he ran track at school, but an angry man with a shot gun can motivate the runner in just about anybody. I was doing my best to keep up and was only a few yards behind him when Taylor aimed the gun up towards the sky and fired off a couple of rounds. At the sound of the gunfire, I fell and screamed, "He got me. Stop, Jim, help me." Those words seemed to light a fire under Jim and he ran even harder.

Now came the time for Joe Boy Barnett to play his next part in our grand charade. A hundred yards down the lane, Joe jumped out from the bushes holding his shotgun and yelled, "Don't worry Daddy, I'll get him," and fired a shot in the air. Now, of course, poor Jim knew for an absolute fact beyond any doubt that he was as good as dead either way he went down the road. His only hope to stay alive, his only option, was to head out into the dark field which, at that particular part of the pasture, sported a bumper crop of prickly pear cactus and short thorny mesquite trees. If you've never seen the thorns on a Mesquite, imagine two to three-inch-long thorns springing up every few inches along every branch. In the darkness they act like little knives reaching out to stab you mercilessly.

After a couple of minutes the three of us converged on the spot where Jim had left the road. Mr. Taylor and Joe Boy shined flashlights and all of us yelled at Jim that it was a joke. Then I took a couple of flashlight and wandered into the shrubs, carefully, until I caught up with poor Jim. He had cactus needles sticking through his trousers up to his knees, looking for all the world like he'd lost a fight with a rabid porcupine. His nice new shirt had tears from the Mesquite thorns. In a few places, he had trickles of blood seeping from the deeper thorn pricks.

I gave him one of the flashlights and helped him make his way out of the brambles and up to the farm house. Inside we took a pair of pliers and, over the next half an hour, pulled out all the bigger cactus needles. Of course, that's when Jim learned that Mr. Taylor was a bachelor and there were no girls.

Jim didn't speak to me for over a week, glaring angrily when we saw each other. As the scrapes and cuts in his skin healed, he started coming around, eventually admitting it was a pretty fine prank. Two weeks later, he and I were sitting together at the soda fountain when we met a new guy, Billy Smith, who was spending July with the Johnsons. After we were acquainted, Jim appeared to get a sudden inspiration, an epiphany. He winked at me and turned to our new friend. "Hey, Billy, you like girls?"

Richard Brown is an award-winning author with publications ranging from technical articles on cooling systems for nuclear power plants to novels, poems and children's stories. Please enjoy this short story based on true events. Jack Griffin and Joe Barnett were real people who shared their past with Richard, who hopes he relayed the joy they expressed when they recounted these memories from their youth.

The Great Go-Kart Katastrophe of 1959

Ryan McSwain

They don't call my hometown Flatland for nothing. My mom used to say the ground was so flat, it needed a tablecloth. You could put a red India-rubber ball on the sidewalk, and it wouldn't roll until you kicked it. People tell you the best thing about Flatland is the sunsets, but the best thing is that nothing rolls away when you aren't looking.

But there are exceptions to every rule, especially in Flatland, Texas. We lived in a nice enough neighborhood, with houses built after the war and plenty of kids. Abbott Street, the street I grew up on, was the eastern boundary of town back then. If you looked on a map, everything past us was labeled Here Be Dragons, except for a little spot set aside for the Woods. Somehow, Abbott Street had the only slope in Flatland. We tried figuring out how one end was higher than the other, but it was like those M.C. Escher stairs. If you went one block over, you could walk back to the top without going uphill. That modest mountain was the only place in Flatland for sledding; when the white fell, kids hiked for miles to slide past my front door.

But it wasn't winter, not then. It was summer, the summer of 1959. We were twelve years old and the manager had just kicked us out of Mortimer's Department Store, the only air-conditioned oasis we had left.

"You should've left those marbles in the bags." Ben wiped the sweat from his smooth brow with a bandana. "I told you a million times, leave those blasted marbles in the bags."

John kicked a rock as we walked down the neighborhood sidewalk. "I opened up a few bags, so what? I wasn't gonna steal any. I just wanted them all to be red, including the shooter. I ain't never had a red shooter before. If I'm paying a whole dime, I'm getting a red shooter."

"But you don't even have a dime," I said. "We're broke, remember?"

"I'd have figured it out, Richie. I always figure it out, don't I?"

"Except when you don't," Ben said, which got the two of us giggling. Ben was built like a refrigerator, so when he got to laughing, it was like a dozen people had the belly laughs all at once.

"You Bozos shut up!" John hated being laughed at, even if we didn't mean anything by it. "I don't see you geniuses coming up with any ideas. If I'd gotten those marbles, at least we could play."

I gasped for breath. "I've got marbles—"

"I only play with *red* marbles!" John turned to storm off, but then we heard the sound. A buzzing—no, not a buzzing, a roar. The monster barreled down the sidewalk. I ended up in the road, skinning my palms something terrible, while Ben and John ended up in the garbage cans.

The go-kart skidded to a stop, and Doug McKenzie and Harvey Owens jumped out. Doug and Phil weren't bad guys, just more full of themselves than John. As soon as they saw we were okay, they started laughing like Sergeant Bilko's studio audience. "The look on your faces!" Harvey howled.

Ben shook the banana peel off his head and jumped out of the garbage. "Are you crazy?" He grabbed the two boys by their collars. "You could've killed us!"

"Hey, Richie!" Doug's voice carried a hint of panic. "Call off your gorilla! We didn't do it on purpose. We lost control, that's all!"

I put a hand on Ben's shoulder. "C'mon, man. Between the two of them, they don't have enough brains to knock around."

As Ben lowered them to the ground, John gave their go-kart tire a kick. "Where'd you get the motor for this thing anyway?" He looked like Mr. Toad, getting his first look at a motor car.

"From my dad's old lawn mower." Harvey straightened his collar and slicked his hair back into place. "We call her Little Queenie. The bike chain keeps slipping off, but we got her up to thirty miles an hour."

"That's bull." But Ben's eyes were taking on the same glazed look as John's.

Doug snorted. "Queenie'll go faster than anything you guys could build, that's for sure."

"Wanna bet?" John said.

I knew where this was headed. "Wait a minute—"

"What ya got in mind?" Doug never turned down a bet in his life. I once saw him drink the liquid out of a magic eight ball. His mom made him go to the doctor, and rumor had it he erupted like Old Faithful. The walls, the carpet, the nurse, everything was stained mystical blue.

I frantically waved my hands at John, but he was already speaking. "Bet you a dollar we can make a faster car. We'll race you."

Doug reached out his hand.

I lunged, but the toe of my Jumping Jacks caught on the curb. By the time I cleared the birdies away, Doug and John were shaking on it. Before John released the other boy's hand, I made an addition to the wager. "It has to be down the hill on Abbott Street!"

By the sacred rules, negotiations could continue until the handshake ended. Doug looked at John, and John squeezed his hand tight. "That okay with you?"

"Queenie can beat you anywhere." But Doug looked worried, like he'd just been tricked but didn't know how.

We ran all the way to Ben's back yard. Once we jumped the chain link fence, Ben laid into John. "You numbskull! You're crazy if you think we can race those guys!"

"I got carried away. We'll just have to find our own lawn mower motor."

"Every kid in town wants a motor like that!" Ben shoved him. "If we could find one, don't you think we'd already have it? Heck, we don't even have a dollar to lose!"

"I'll figure it out!"

"Oh, you'll figure it out, you'll figure it out. John, when have you ever figured anything out? It's always Richie!"

"Yeah? Who figured out how to break into the school?"

"Richie."

"Then who got us out of the bomb shelter?"

"Who do you think?"

John searched for another argument. "Okay, jeez. Richie, you got any ideas? Or at least a dollar stashed somewhere?"

"We just need kids." I tried to sound more confident than I felt. "All the kids we can get."

A week later at high noon, children lined both sides of Abbott Street, with even a few teenagers wading among the cap-gun cowboys and little girls holding winking dollies above their heads for a better look. Most of the crowd, I'm sure, hoped for the inevitable disaster. Doug McKenzie and Harvey Owens waited at the high end of the street, just before the steep drop, pretending to tinker with Little Queenie. As we rolled around the corner, Doug and Harvey laughed so hard they had to lean on their vehicle for support.

We'd scavenged every piece of wood in the neighborhood. Our go-kart looked like a half-finished tree fort, minus the structural integrity. Ben christened it the Flying Fortress, after his favorite plastic model kit. The Fortress had four wheels of varying sizes, a brake made from a fireplace shovel, and a rope for steering. But what set the Fortress apart from every go-kart ever made by thinking individuals was the second story, accessible by ladder. We'd tried painting the behemoth red, but ran out of paint halfway through. We didn't have access to any safety features in 1959, otherwise we'd have thrown them in too. Our own mob of kids were pushing it to the starting line, and I fit the wheel chocks into place. We'd put so much cooking grease on the wheel bearings, I feared the wind would push it down the hill without us.

Doug took a walk around the Flying Fortress. "Who are all these kids? Your pit crew?" Instead of answering, they climbed onto their spots on the kart. When Doug realized what they were doing, his giggles took a powder. "Wait a minute! That ain't fair!"

John hopped in the driver's seat, looking smug. "The bet didn't say anything about how many kids could ride along. What do you care, anyway? They'll just slow us down." But Doug and Harvey looked doubtful as they took turns trying to start their old lawnmower engine.

My plan was a simple one, as evidenced by the crayon diagrams that guided the creation of the Flying Fortress. We would pile as many kids as we could in front of the back axle, giving us the highest possible momentum. With a little luck—and as long as the wheels spun freely and the kart held together—we stood a chance of beating Doug and Harvey.

Estimates vary as to the number of passengers aboard the Flying Fortress. I would've sworn there were nine of us, because I wasn't sure how we'd split the dollar if we won. But Ben argued for twelve. Months later, John literally swore on a Bible that there were fifteen. By the end of the summer, every kid in the neighborhood claimed to in that race, maybe every kid in Flatland. The rubberneckers watching must have been an illusion.

John was the driver, because of course he was, with kids huddled behind him. Jason Ito was lying down on the second floor with a few other boys and girls. Ben held onto the passenger side wall with more pieces of human ballast. I was clinging to the driver's side, so that I could yell at John. It was time for me to be more assertive. Casey Kimball, all curls and red polka dots, held onto the rail beside me. We'd asked her little brother, who still owed us a favor, but she wouldn't let him go without her. I tried talking her out of it, but no dice. Her warm hand next to mine was a source of anxiety greater than the suicide mission we would soon undertake.

At least a few individuals under twelve weren't on the Fortress, because it was their job to pull out the wheel chocks. A few of the bigger kids agreed to push start the car, including everyone's favorite bully, Frankie Lee. Guess he decided if anyone was going to have the honor of sending me to my death, it should be him.

Middle-school heart-throb Dawn Pearson volunteered to start the race, and John blushed so hard I thought his head would pop. She raised the metal cap gun, my own Hubley Atomic Disintegrator, and pulled the trigger. The pinch of gunpowder, wedged inside a red paper ribbon, exploded. We were off.

Frankie and his goons came through, shoving hard enough to get us going. Once we hit the incline, my stomach floated, just like the drop on the carnival's roller coaster. In John's eyes, I witnessed abject fear, greater than when we stayed up to watch *Invaders from Mars*. Cognizant of my own mortality, I placed my hand over Casey Kimball's and made a wish.

Everything happened quickly after that. Most kids believed Doug and Harvey's chain snapped, then they lost control, then I yelled "Brake!" I've run over the events in my mind many times, and I can't be sure. It makes sense for a standpoint of causality; the lost chain caused the other kart to career into the Flying Fortress, exploding the wheelbarrow tire on our front driver's side, which triggered my command to stop. But I might have panicked upon realizing we were winning—and still picking up speed. I wonder if it was my shout that caused Doug to jerk his steering wheel, bringing about our own doom. But for the purpose of this story, we'll side with the majority.

Little Queenie rammed the front corner of the Flying Fortress. The tire exploded and the exposed wheel hit the gravel, showering Ben with sparks. He buried his face in his arm and tightened his grip.

A distant voice called out, and I assume it was my own. "Brake!"

John grabbed the fireplace shovel. It wedged against the spinning axle for a moment, and my heart sang. But then the shovel snapped, leaving John holding a useless iron bar.

"Brake, John!" Ben yelled through the haze of fireworks. "Brake!"

John waved the broken shaft. "Ain't got no—"

At the sound of the crunch, every adult on the block paused, peeked out their windows, and went right back to what they were doing.

The Flying Fortress possessed no speedometer, so it's impossible to know how fast we were going when we hit the curb. The busted tire must have slowed us down, but you wouldn't have known it from the impact. Nine or twelve or fifteen or a hundred kids were in the air. I can see that moment like it's still burned onto the back of my eyelids. Casey floating in the air like an angel. Ben spinning like an acrobat, his shirt covered in tiny burns from the sparks. John, upside down in the sky, still clutching the remains of the brake.

We bounced and skidded. When I sat up, pieces of the Flying Fortress were still falling from the heavens. Casey was laughing harder than Woody Woodpecker, and Ben ran through every combination of swear words he knew. They lived.

"John? You okay?" I stood, the ground swaying under me. Looking around, I didn't see brains splattered anywhere. Our fellow idiots looked punch drunk, but everyone was moving. I found John, face down in the grass. In my mind, I pictured the brake handle stuck through him like a pin through a butterfly. I rolled him, and he looked up at me. "Lost a tooth."

"Tooth fairy or the other kind?" I asked.

"Tooth fairy." He spit the tiny molar into his hand. "Richie, no more bets for me. And next time you drive."

"I'm fine in the background. Ben keeps his cool, let's make him drive."

"Good call. Help me remember, about the bets."

"You got it, buddy."

Jason Ito got the worst of it. He spent the rest of the summer showing off his broken arm. By the time school started, his cast had more signatures than a petition to bring back *The Mickey Mouse Club*. As for the one dollar bet, it was agreed that neither Little Queenie nor the Flying Fortress finished the race, so everyone was even steven.

It turned out John didn't get permission to borrow the fireplace shovel or the wheels off his dad's push mower. While he spent the next few days grounded, Ben and I canvased the neighborhood for a set of red marbles, complete with shooter. We hoped they would keep John out of trouble.

And they did, for a few days. But that's another story.

Ryan McSwain lives in Amarillo, Texas, with his wife and their two children. Ryan spends his days playing with his kids, writing, and wallowing in nostalgia. He's published two novels, Monsters All the Way Down *and* Four Color Bleed. *If you'd like to change reality, please check with him first—he's currently living his best possible timeline.*
Website: ryanmcswain.com
Twitter: @ryanmcswain
Amazon Author Page: amazon.com/Ryan-McSwain/e/B00KOV2FXA

A WWII Submariner:

Jerome Paul Fojtik

Frank Carden

"As British airmen are credited with saving Britain in those critical days after Dunkirk, so our gallant submarine personnel filled the breach after Pearl Harbor, and can claim credit, not only for holding the line, but also for carrying the war to the enemy while our shattered forces repaired damages. Because of the complete absence of publicity regarding our submarine operations during the war, and due to an understandable letdown in public interest in news following the surrender of the Japanese in Tokyo Bay, the American public is largely unaware of their great debt to that relative small but closely knit force which had, at its peak, not more than 4,000 officers and 46,000 men, of which number some 16,000 actually manned the submarines."

Fleet Admiral Chester W. Nimitz, US Navy

Pearl Harbor

Thursday, December 11, 1941

Four days after the Japanese attack, the submarine USS *Gudgeon* (SS-211) got underway from Pearl Harbor. The sub sailed past the smoking ruins of U.S. ships. The sneak attack by Japanese forces had devastated the Navy's warships and the Army Air Corp's planes. The blackened hulks of four battleships lay silent in dark waters, mute testimony to the effectiveness of Sunday morning's attack. The *Arizona*—33,000 tons, 600 feet long, 100 feet wide—lay with her keel pushing against the sandy bottom. Fourteen feet below the water's surface, her main gun mounts, each weighing 93 tons, were invisible under murky, oil-coated water.

Entombed in her flooded compartments were the bodies of 1,150 sailors.

The men on the bridge of the submarine *Gudgeon* said nothing, nor could they look away. In the air was the stench of oil, charred wood, and burned and rotting bodies. Small boats slowly plied the harbor water, stopping to pull oil-coated, bloated bodies from the water. For several days, most men had been working to rescue any wounded, taking them to the overflowing hospitals.

Gudgeon, loaded with torpedoes and food for the crew, headed for the waters of Imperial Japan 3,400 miles away to conduct the first offensive strike by U.S. forces in the war. It would be the first combat patrol by an American submarine in WWII to reach the waters of the Empire.

The first of many. By war's end, the sub force comprised about four percent of Navy personnel and had sunk a major portion of the Japanese tonnage destroyed by the United States. The submarine force paid the price. Of the almost 200 subs that participated in the Pacific war, fifty-two did not return. Some 3,500 officers and men remain on Eternal Patrol. The men who served on submarines received combat patrol pins.

The submarine force became known as the Silent Service. Submerged in the water's depths, they moved silently to attack. Neither the sailors on patrol nor the top brass sending them out talked about the subs for fear the information would filter back to the Japanese. Certainly, no one talked to journalists eager for any stories of heroic actions that would sell papers as well as boost morale on the American home front. Silent Service was a fitting title. The men with the pins never talked about their experience, not to others, not to each other. For over six decades, they remained silent. This nonfiction piece is the story of one submarine sailor, Jerome Fojtik.

Motor Machinist Mate Second Class SS

San Francisco, California

Monday, September 17, 1944, Thursday, December 11, 1941

"More coffee?" Ann asked.

"Yeah, please." Jerry looked at his new wife, at her full red lips, her green eyes, the long eyelashes. She lifted the small pot he had brewed and poured his mug full. When he touched her hand curved around the handle of the pot, she smiled, but barely. Moments earlier, she had come from the Navy administration building on Treasure Island where she worked, and had just removed the jacket of her WAVE uniform. The starched white blouse was tucked into her dark blue skirt, showing off a narrow waist.

"Just five more days. That's all we have," she said. "Then you'll be going back to the war on *Halibut*. Her tenth patrol. Her tenth!"

He glanced out the window at the water of the Pacific that had turned an indigo blue as the sun slipped beneath the horizon.

"We never hear, but we know. Subs don't always come back." In her eyes, tears reflected the last rays of the sun.

"I have your two-week anniversary wedding present," he said.

She sat the pot back on the two-burner without looking and stood motionless.

"I've transferred from *Halibut* to *Scamp*. The transfer was approved today. *Scamps's* going on her next war patrol three weeks after *Halibut*. That gives us an extra twenty-one days."

"Twenty-one days. Oh, oh, you are my world, my life." She spun and sat down in his lap, burying her face against his. Her warm tears fell on his cheek. Jerry took a deep breath, folded his arms around her, but said nothing. From his birthplace in Shiner, Texas to Denver, and then to the submarines, had been an exciting ride. But nothing like the emotions he was experiencing with Ann. He looked at their wedding photo on the table, at the lovely white orchid in her jacket lapel, at her heart-stopping smile. He loved her completely.

Four weeks later, with Fojtik on board, *Scamp* left Pearl Harbor on October 16, 1944, on her war patrol. North of Iwo Jima, 100 miles south of Tokyo, the sub acknowledged receiving a radio message on November 9, 1944. She was never heard from again. Fojtik was twenty-three.

A colleague, Tudor Davis, who served on *Halibut* with Fojtik, told me about the transfer and result. The story of these two people, wonderfully in love, seemed to me the quintessential love story of WWII. I looked up *Scamp* on the website of lost subs and saw that wonderful photo, posted below. I knew this beautiful, sad story had to be told. When I finished writing the story, down to the loss of *Scamp*, I thought that was the end. Not quite.

To use the photo in this piece, I needed to find the person who had submitted the photo to the website. I contacted Master Chief Charles Hinman, the man in charge of the submarine museum in Hawaii and that website. He was extremely cooperative and gave me the name of Fojtik's niece who had submitted the photo from her family album. He emailed the niece, Jacqueline Slaughter, informing her I would be in contact. After one email exchange, she graciously gave me permission to use the photo.

Through emails, I asked if she had any information on Ann Fojtik. She said when she was very young, she had visited Ann in Los Alamos, New Mexico with her mother and father, Jerome's younger brother. And that was the extent of her knowledge of Ann. But Jackie Slaughter started looking at records on Ann Fojtik. She found that Ann died in 1988 at age 67. She was interred in the Fort Logan National Cemetery, Denver Colorado, a National Military Cemetery located on a mesa surrounded by distant mountains. Row upon row of white headstone punctuate green trees and grass, enveloped by the Colorado blue sky.

Jackie continued researching records on Ann at Los Alamos. Many engineers and scientist worked in Los Alamos. Most, at that time, were men. So I figured that Ann had remarried and moved to that small town, but Jackie found out otherwise. Ann Fojtik, that beautiful woman, had not remarried. For the rest of her life, she remained true to the one man she loved, that twenty-three year old sailor who had sailed away, never to return.

Jerry Fojtik and wife, Ann.

Painting the Town Red

A Salute to our Veterans

Phyliss Miranda

I remember the cold and blustery day when I closed my eyes and said a little prayer that He would give me the strength to get through the task at hand.

It was extremely hard to sort through my Aunt Bobbie's possessions following her death, particularly since it was more like sorting through two generation's keepsakes. My family has never been very good at throwing out our "stuff," so there was a mixture of both Aunt Bobbie's precious memories mingled with those of my grandmother. Thank goodness we are packrats, or I wouldn't have this story to share with you.

I found "the letter" in the family Bible—you know the one that everyone has . . . gold leaf nearly worn off and the binding so fragile that it's held together with masking tape. Ours has silver duct tape, too. The book protects an assortment of obituaries, wedding and birth announcements, and other newspaper clippings wedged between the pages. I picked up Granny's handwritten recipe for Louisiana Pecan Pie. It sounds like a strange place to keep a recipe, but not if you had known my Aunt Bobbie.

Although I'd thumbed through the family Bible many times as I grew up, I'd never noticed "the letter." After keeping it secure for all those years, did my aunt move it to the one place she was sure I'd find it? I don't know. But, I do know with Aunt Bobbie, everything had a reason.

The three pages are as yellowed with age as the memories inked on them. It's written in a precise yet manly flourish with a black fountain pen scripted on light weight "air mail" stationery.

As I slowly unfolded the fragile pages, an odd sensation of calmness and serenity settle around me. I demanded that my emotions take a back seat and allow me privacy to read the letter, thus getting to know my Uncle Vick, Aunt Bobbie's brother.

July 29, 1944

Dearest Bobbie,

I wish it were possible to talk to you and tell you what I have to say.

I'm telling you so you can tell Mom. I don't know how she will take it and I don't want her to be alone when she gets the news. I want you to see that she doesn't worry about me because there is no cause for it. I am in good condition now but I was wounded worse than I let you know.

I am perfectly content and quite happy. The only thing I regret is having to leave the Marine Corps. My days in the service are few but I am happy that my discharge is honorable.

I landed on the Island of Saipan with the assault wave. I made it almost through the campaign but my luck ran out and I got in front of a Jap Machine gun. I took four bullets in my left leg and one in my left arm. My arm is completely healed but I wasn't so lucky with the leg. This is what I've been trying to say. To save my life they had to remove my left leg. In other words I only have one leg. Don't feel sorry for me and don't worry.

Today thanks to science a man doesn't have to worry because they have artificial legs that a man can walk on just as normal as ever. He can dance, work, walk, run and do most anything else any other man can do. I don't feel badly at all. I take it as just something that had to happen and I thank God I am alive.

I'll be in the states soon. I will be in California for some time. After the leg is healed it takes a long time to get the stump tough enough for the leg to be attached. But I think I will get to come home for a while. Possibly in about three months. It won't be the home coming I wanted but we are going to have lots of fun aren't we? We can paint any town just as red as anyone else.

I haven't told Naomi (his wife) yet and I don't want Mom to tell her. That is my job. How I do it is something I haven't figured out as yet.

Don't write anymore until you hear from me again. Tell Mom the same thing. I expect to have a new address and it takes mail too long to catch up with me.

Keep Mom from worrying about me. Keep your chin up and we'll all be happy.

I have to close now. I'll be thinking of you and loving you,

Always, your Bud,
Vick

P.S: Tell Dad first. Maybe he can help. I'll tell more next time. Love always, Vick

Through blurry eyes and swallowing a lump in my throat much too big to go down, I read the letter twice before returning the yellowed pages to its resting place. The most appropriate place I knew to stow the treasure . . . our family Bible.

The letter had been written sixty years ago, in a faraway country, by a Marine fighting for our democracy.

Today I forced myself to reread the letter, as I prepared to share his story. I thought about the hundreds of thousands of other servicemen that sent home similar letters.

In reflection, I didn't get to know Uncle Vick while he was alive. His pictures show a handsome man, full of life and laughter. The family storytellers told of how he survived that horrid day lying amongst a pile of fallen American heroes and praying to God. I wonder if he prayed for survival or for a quick death? Only God knows.

I'm sorry that I missed the opportunity to really get to know him, but in 1952 God called him home earlier than the family planned. Uncle Vick was laid to rest at the age of 33 in the National Cemetery in Fresno, California.

In the six decades since Uncle Vick poured out his heart and soul and his fears and love to his sister, my aunt, we've seen the end to World War II, the Korean conflict, Vietnam, Desert Storm, September 11th, and the war in Iraq.

For centuries our servicemen have given their limbs and their lives so fellow countryman can enjoy democracy and have the opportunity to ". . . paint any town just as red as anyone else."

I'm thankful, Aunt Bobbie, for leaving your brother's letter in a place where you knew I'd find it. Because God answered the prayers of Victor C. Johnson, U.S.M.C., on that dreadful day on the Island of Saipan, I now know my uncle—a man of courage and convictions, a heroic, honorable Marine who did not look back in regret for an instant after losing a limb for his country, a husband, brother, and son with compassion and tremendous love for his family and country.

Prologue

On a special spring day in San Antonio while watching my grandchildren play, my cell phone rang. On the other end of the line a woman asked if I was Phyliss Pannier Miranda, and I said yes. She asked if I had an aunt named Bobbie and if my mother's name was Ruth. I confirmed. Then she asked if I had an Uncle Vic. I paused and slowly answered, "Yes." She then said, "Hello, I'm your cousin Vicky."—my Uncle Vic's daughter.

Vicki and I hadn't seen one another since we were small and her family moved to California. While doing family genealogy she had come across my information. To my surprise, she had not seen the above story on my web-site and I talked her through finding it. I listened as she said over and over, "That's my daddy!" I'm thrilled to say we've forged a bond and are real family now, all because of her daddy's letter saved in the family Bible.

Crippled

Sandy Haney

Floor-length strands of beads hung in the doorway of my bedroom, and I scowled at the long-haired brunette who placed them there. My nine-year-old heart puzzled over the necessity of my beloved uncle's new girlfriend, and why playing baseball with me wasn't sufficient for him. I understood Robbie turning down an offer to play for the minor leagues to serve his country, but if the Vietnam War had taken its toll on his first marriage, why would he want to marry again? My youth couldn't grasp the extent to which the war's trauma crippled my uncle's mind. His first wife grew so lonely awaiting her sailor's return that, though they had a baby, she fell in love with, and left him for, another man. However, what I didn't understand was that this rejection, combined with the crippling images of war, left Robbie thoroughly incapacitated. His new love interest, Dianna, was a way of finally moving on and finding hope in the future.

Robbie's parents (my grandparents/guardians) experienced a horrific nightmare in those dark days of war. They understood Robbie's job to be that of lifting and loading the bodies (or what was left of them) of U.S. casualties for transport.

One of these men had not yet died, which shocked Robbie when he felt the collar of his uniform suddenly clutched by the dying man's hand. The man's pleading eyes searched Robbie's face as he gasped his final breath. What Robbie didn't realize was that the man had snatched his necklace-like dog tag in the process. It ended up being the only piece of identifying information officials were able to find on the deceased man. The officials naturally assumed the man's identity was Robbie's, which led them to call and give my grandparents the information that their son had died. Grief-stricken wasn't a strong enough term to describe their reaction.

Unbeknownst to my grandparents, Robbie was admitted to a military hospital in Germany with a nervous breakdown. My grandparents were flown there to verify the identity of someone claiming to be their son. My grandmother, who had fainted when she received the call about her son's death, passed out again when she saw that he was, in fact, alive!

Shortly after his military discharge and return home, my uncle had an unfortunate encounter with a rabid cat. At his first medical appointment concerning this incident, he met the receptionist, Dianna. After a few minutes getting acquainted, Robbie asked the long-haired brunette if she'd like to join him for supper that evening at a French restaurant. She suspiciously asked the name of the restaurant, to which my uncle responded, "Jacques in the Box!"

Intrigued by his unpretentious manner and charming sense of humor, Dianna accepted the supper invitation. She found Robbie so easy to talk to that she agreed to see him again. They had brief but frequent visits at the clinic as a result of his rabies regimen and found subsequent lengthier opportunities to spend time together. I've never known my uncle to cry easily, but Dianna fell in love with him when she shared her abusive childhood and he cried. His tender heart, which he considered a curse while serving our country, proved to be a blessing in his personal life.

The unconventional Dianna soon became my aunt, and while hanging beads in my bedroom doorway made me scratch my head, I came to know her as the one person that could make my beloved uncle truly happy. That was worth more to my nine-year-old heart than all our days spent playing baseball together. The young sailor mentally crippled by rejection and war had finally found unequivocal acceptance and love.

Blue Roses at the Wartburg

Cheryle Cooper

Claudette snatched the eggshell-colored skirt-suit that hung at the back of her closet, and pressed it, hanger and all, against her body. With serious skepticism, she stared at her grainy reflection, suddenly no longer a fan of the pleats at the bottom. The tone seemed way off, as if the jacket had faded. She turned from side-to-side, examining. "What is the point?" she mumbled to herself.

Defeated, she tossed the outfit into a heaping pile with the rest of the rejects and flopped down hard on the edge of the bed. She shook, sobbing uncontrollably. At that moment, she needed to pray. Maybe that was her problem—not enough time spent in the Word and prayer.

Regardless, it should *not* have been *this* difficult to pick out something decent to wear for a lunch date with her husband—a man she still loved, even though lately things had grown distant and strained between them. So much so that her husband, Kirk, took on legal projects that kept him away from home months at a time. He was a partner in a successful, mid-sized law firm and Claudette assumed his initial rationale for extended travel was rooted in that old adage: absence makes the heart grow fonder. Of course, everybody knew the flip side: out of sight; out of mind. She was crushed to discover after nearly 26-years of marriage and four children later they had fallen *noticeably* into the latter category. This new reality was about as welcome as belated frost on spring lilies.

At first, the space they needed to diffuse some of the tension worked out well. Kirk dutifully flew back home every two weeks from his detail in Washington, D.C.—spending enough time to enjoy some neutral things like dinner out or the symphony or maybe even an art show, but not enough time to waste haggling over their differences—differences that came about when Claudette became a Christian. She started going to Bible study and gradually acquired new friends. She had new interests. New likes. New dislikes. A new heart, a new mind—a new passion for God her husband could not comprehend. All this newness took its toll.

"I'm telling you, Bud, the wife and I are going in different directions," she overheard him confiding to a friend. It broke her heart to hear him say that, but the truth was undeniable.

By January things had come to a head, and Kirk's visits home dwindled to once a month or less. His usual excuse was he couldn't get away. "Hon, we're really getting hammered on this project. I'll have to see about next week," he would tell her. By the time he did manage to get home, he would fly into town on a Friday night and depart on a Sunday afternoon, usually too jetlagged to do anything but nap in between.

Worse than that, a rumor circulated that he had been seen having frequent lunches with a female clerk at a DuPont Circle café. The rumor reached all the way back to their home town of Lubbock, Texas. It didn't help that the young woman in question was smart and attractive. When Claudette confronted him, he vigorously denied doing anything untoward. "She's been helping us on some of our intellectual property cases. That's all."

But Claudette did not know what to believe. She felt she hardly knew Kirk, anymore. Maybe he was telling the truth. Whatever the case, the damage was done and the distasteful hearsay caused the chasm to widen, creating a palpable impasse between them.

So naturally, when he called to invite her to do lunch, she became instantly alarmed. After all, for weeks he'd been claiming to be "so tied up with work." But now he wanted to *talk*. Claudette suspected his real reason was to discuss a legal separation. Had it really come to this? Tormented, she replayed their phone conversation in her head.

"Lunch?" she asked under her breath.

"Yes," he said sounding more matter-of-fact and energized than he had in a while. "I'm coming in Monday night for a quick break. But no worries, I booked a room at the West End. That way, I don't disrupt you and the kids' schedule."

How big of you, she wanted to say. "I see."

"Yeah... Anyway... I was thinking we could go to the Wartburg. We haven't been there in years."

"The Wartburg?" *That hole in the wall*, she thought. Well, it wasn't exactly a hole in the wall. It just exuded "baby boom era" charm and the nostalgic ambience so popular in Lubbock's Depot District.

"Oh, I heard they've spruced it up quite a bit these days," he said, as if he knew exactly what she was thinking. "I can't promise you they got rid of those tacky blue roses in the vestibule, though. Remember those? But you've got to admit they have *the* best chicken pot pie in the entire Panhandle."

Claudette slowly rose from the bed and wiped her face with the back of her hand. There was nothing more to deliberate. They were having lunch tomorrow at one—and that was that. She collected each item of clothing off the floor and gathered them up in her arms. What difference did it make what she wore if her husband planned to leave her? The tears rolled down her face; this time she bowed her head and prayed.

Tuesday morning started somber and overcast. But, by the afternoon, the day had transformed into a bright and beautiful 75°, despite the infamous whipping winds of the Texas Plains. Unable to completely shake her uneasiness, Claudette arose with a stronger resolve than she had the day before. On her way to the restaurant, she recalled the words from Psalm 16:11 that she had read first thing that morning: *'Thou wilt shew me the path of life: in Thy presence is fulness of joy; at Thy right hand there are pleasures for evermore."* Amen! No matter what, she believed His presence was all the strength she needed.

The Wartburg was a time-honored fixture in Lubbock. It sat near the Cactus Theatre and fit right in with the other dusty establishments and few refurbished sports bars along Buddy Holly

Avenue. Claudette and Kirk had not been there in years. The last time, their youngest son had been only two-years old. Now he was twelve. For the life of her, she could not figure out why Kirk wanted to eat there—except, hands down, they had *the* best chicken pot pie on the planet. Ironically, it was also where they had their official first date, twenty-nine years ago.

When Claudette walked in, she did not see Kirk anywhere. *Ah ha! I beat him here!* She relished the thought. However, scanning the foyer, she couldn't miss those iconic blue roses, which were on display in bulky glass vases. Dyed to perfection, she could see. But, to her eyes, they did not look the least bit tacky. In fact, they looked vibrant and beautiful.

"Will you be okay over here, ma'am?" The waitress asked, seating Claudette in a booth where she had a clear view of the entrance.

Nodding, with a smile, Claudette answered, "Yes. Thank you. My husband should be along any minute." *Perfect! I'll be able to see him when he walks in.*

Like clockwork, Kirk—all six feet two inches of him—strode in with unmistakable purpose at around two minutes to one. He walked quickly past the waitress and was soon face-to-face with Claudette. "Is this seat taken?" he asked, smiling ever so slightly.

There was a distinctive playfulness in his tone. Maybe this lunch date wasn't going to be the gloom and doom session she had previously imagined. She smiled, unable to resist his striking sea-green eyes and motioned him to sit down.

Since business was slow, the waitress took their order right away and was back promptly with their meal—chicken pot pie. In between chews, they laughed about those crazy blue roses and bantered about how the kids were doing. Kirk even mentioned, more than once, how beautiful Claudette looked. If only he knew how much time she spent agonizing over what to wear, before finally deciding on the printed red dress. Claudette realized the small talk was over when Kirk gingerly pushed his plate away. "That was good," he said, smiling at her.

"Yes," she whispered, staring down at a small stain on the Calico tablecloth.

"Umm," he started, clearing his throat. "I decided I'm coming home at the end of May. I already talked to Rory about ending my part on this assignment. We've worked it out so that Dave Simmons, the other partner, can finish out the contract negotiations. It's a royalty dispute. Kinda messy stuff. I have a few odds and ends to tie up. But, after that, I'm outta there."

Claudette heard the words, all right—but struggled to compute. The end of May was only a few weeks away. Five, to be exact. "What? Why?"

"Well . . ." He shifted his weight from side-to-side. "For one thing, my company needs me here. A ten-month stint out of town is a long time to be gone from the office. Too long." Then, gazing off, he lowered his voice and confessed, "I need to be home with you all, Claudie. I want us to work things out. I won't pretend that I understand everything. But, I'm certainly willing to try."

Don't break down in this place, Claudette thought to herself. *Don't break down.* Still, she felt her lower lip quiver. Taking a deep breath, she stared at Kirk. She couldn't remember a time when he looked more vulnerable. No question about it, he was still the handsome man she married all those years ago. She mustered up the courage and asked him, "What happened?"

"What do mean, what happened?" he asked, wrinkling up his face.

"Why'd you change your mind?" she said. "I thought you loved the new projects and the change of pace."

It took him a while to answer. He cleared his throat again, and said, "You know I don't believe in dream interpretations or anything foolish like that. But . . ." He stopped, inhaled deeply, and continued. "But about three or four weeks ago, I had a dream—actually a nightmare—that I lost you. Really lost you. It was scary. I couldn't believe how real it seemed."

"Lost me?" she repeated. "How?"

After another deep breath, Kurt explained. "Well . . . in this dream you were telling the kids that you needed to pick up something from the store. And next thing, there was this horrific accident. Lights. Blood. Crashing. I mean, I can still hear it ringing in my ears now. The police on the scene had pronounced you dead. I was standing in the distance, yelling and screaming, but nobody heard me. No one. I can't tell you how real it felt. I actually woke up drenched in sweat."

For a few seconds they exchanged no words. Claudette felt the heaviness in the air and she could see on her husband's face that he was visibly jolted. Then, he spoke in a voice that cracked: "I can't shake the idea that maybe God was trying to get my attention."

God? Did he just say *God?* Now, she wondered if *she* was the one dreaming. "Wow," she muttered.

"You know," he went on, his voice still cracking, "You have to believe me, Claudie, nothing happened in D.C. Nothing. I would never, ever do that to you—or *to us*. But I'm sorry I gave you cause to doubt me."

Unable to speak or hold back tears, Claudette nodded.

"Can I get these out of your way?" The waitress's voice boomed, temporarily shattering the tenderness and intensity of the moment. Thankfully, the lady collected the dishes fast and shuffled off to the kitchen.

Kirk reached over and softly squeezed Claudette's hand. "I love you," he said, so low she could barely hear him.

She dabbed her face with the stiff napkin. "I love you, too."

"I don't know," he went on. "The last few weeks have been . . . sort of crazy. A lot of soul searching, I guess. I don't know."

Claudette couldn't help giggling. "Imagine that. A lawyer, lost for words," she teased.

"Yeah, imagine that." He smiled, still holding her hand from across the table. "I've got so much to tell you, that's for sure. But I don't want to do it here." He flagged down the waitress and paid their tab. They stood and held each other tight in a long overdue embrace. Claudette didn't realize how much she missed him nor could she stop the steady stream of tears that tumbled down her face.

Kirk kissed her lightly on her forehead. "How 'bout we grab an Italian ice off of Quaker? You want to?"

"Yes." She felt as if she could float out of there.

Holding hands, they took their time leaving the Wartburg. Claudette was convinced that greasy spoon would forever hold a special place in her heart. But more than anything, she was reaffirmed in the fact that no matter the place and no matter the time, God answers His children's prayers.

Cheryle Cooper lives in Amarillo, Texas where she owns and operates Expert Editing – a home-based writing and editing business. Over the years, Ms. Cooper has had numerous articles and stories published in regional magazines. Now that she has successfully completed a demanding – yet rewarding – stint as a home-school teacher, she is thrilled to be working on her first children's book – along with writing inspirational short-stories and non-fiction articles.

Eighty-Nine Seconds

Mike Akins

Daniel squeezes my hand, our fingers laced, and I smile back. We've been married seven years. We practically lived on love those first years and were too poor and naive to think it could be any different. That it would ever be any different. But as hot as we were for each other, our relationship burned itself out. This trip feels like a last-ditch effort to rekindle that early passion. Maybe that's putting too much pressure on the outcome. Why can't I just relax and enjoy it for what it is?

I feel lost without a little modeling clay underneath my finger nails. I look out the window of the airplane at the cerulean ocean stretching to the horizon, a patchwork of puffy clouds floating lazily below. I want to touch those clouds, run my hands over them, shape them the way I shape a lump of clay with my practiced fingers. The way I sometimes do things with my eyes closed, feeling what belongs and what doesn't. My husband says it must be some sort of magic. But to me it's like breathing, effortless.

"What are you thinking?" Daniel's thumb brushes over mine and I look from the window.

"Nothing," I say, working to turn my thoughts back to the here and now.

He forces a laugh, but at least he's trying. "Your studio can do without you for a week."

"No fair peeking in my head." I offer him a smile. "I guess I can I do without my studio. It's just a week, right?"

Those deep brown eyes say that maybe I *can* do without. They say maybe I can get lost all over again in their depths, the way I did eight years ago when I first met him.

"If I can tear myself away from the office, you can live without your studio."

It does feel like a tearing, a ripping away of some better part of me. "Yeah, I suppose so."

He seems satisfied with that and settles back in his seat. The flight attendant pushes his cart to our row and takes our drink orders, hands Daniel a coke, me a sparkling water. I pull the tray down and set the clear-plastic cup there, watching the bubbles float effortlessly to the top. If only I was as effortless in my life as I am in my art.

"We haven't had a trip together like this in years."

It has been years. I know Daniel's a newly minted lawyer and some long hours are to be expected. But, dammit, I feel like a widow. I'm ashamed to admit it, but I hate him for it, for depriving me of him. This was supposed to get better after law school. Now I see even less of him. I'm tired of sleeping alone.

Before I can settle into this righteous indignation, a niggling voice says I'm just as much to blame. My career has taken off and money is rolling in for commissioned art pieces, and I never miss an opportunity to throw my success in his face. If he is jealous, I've egged him on. Maybe that's why we argue about money all the time, because we're spending *my* money. When I first suggested this trip, he balked at the price. But what's the point of saving for the future when our now is bankrupt? I know we're both better than the two people we've become.

"I'm a little nervous."

He sits up. "Why?"

"I'm worried about us." I see the concern in his eyes and my insides melt. This man sitting next to me looks like the old Daniel. The one who took my breath away, the one whose touch gave me gooseflesh.

"We'll be okay."

That's Daniel. Always so damn confident, bordering on arrogant. Something that I've found, in turns, both irresistible and infuriating.

The airplane bumps over a pocket of turbulence and my stomach does a flip. I brought a book, but I'm too unsettled to read. There's an inflight movie, but I'm not wanting the distraction right now. I want to work through my conflicted emotions.

I pull a lump of playdough out of my bag and knead it with my fingers, start shaping it. This centers me, allows my creative side to come to the fore. It only takes a few minutes for me to know what figure is hiding in the shapeless mass. My breathing slows and my anxiety ebbs as the emerging shape takes precedence. I work quickly. Ten minutes later, a more-than-passable likeness of Daniel sits on the palm of my hand. He's let me have this space, knows better than to intrude when I'm "being creative."

He nudges me with his shoulder. "Seems like a nice fellow."

"You wouldn't like him."

"And why not?" He affects an air of indignation.

"Because I have this Daniel in the palm of my hand." He chuckles at this. "And he'll be there when I need him." I mean it as a joke, but it hits a little too close to home.

I backpedal quickly when I see the genuine hurt on his face. "No. Daniel. I didn't—"

"It's all right." He runs his finger over the other Daniel's hair. "I could learn a lot from this little fellow."

We don't fight. Maybe this trip is exactly what we need. And for the first time in a long while I allow myself to experience a glimmer of hope.

I glance out the window and notice a thin stream of smoke tailing from the engine. Before I can raise an alarm, the engine and part of the wing disappear in an orange fireball and the plane lurches, slamming me to the fuselage. My shoulder howls in pain.

Eighty-nine

I'm yanked the other direction, my seatbelt digging into my thighs. Several people tumble down the aisle, desperately grasping for something to stop their fall. I try to right myself and can't. Outside my window, the sea and sky trade places. My ears are buzzing and when I look at Daniel, he's shouting something.

The world around me is a spinning, roaring blur. The tray table is gone and there's blood on my legs. The oxygen masks swing free where they've deployed but I can still breath. Can still breath. I take a shuddering breath and the gravity of the moment crystalizes.

I'm going to die.

Seventy-eight

Daniel is still shouting. His hands reach for me and he catches me by the shoulders. Blood pours from a cut over his eye. He's saying something, but nothing registers. And then my ears clear. I can hear screaming, the din reminiscent of wounded animals. A sound at once recognizable and alien.

"Are you hurt?"

Daniel has been talking this whole time. He repeats the question, but the question doesn't fit in my brain in a way that makes sense. My shoulder throbs but it doesn't matter. The enormity of a life unlived looms over me and I can feel my sanity sliding.

Seventy

"Look at me!" He squeezes my hurt shoulder and I wince. The pain brings me back to the now. The chaos is incomprehensible. I see the face of the woman in the aisle across from us, and the terror in her eyes must mirror mine. I look down at my hand. The Daniel I made is destroyed. Crushed.

"Don't look anywhere else. Right here."

His face, his beautiful face, comes into focus.

"This is all my fault. I wanted this trip. You shouldn't be here."

He's shaking his head. "There's no place I'd rather be than right here with you."

Sixty-one

There's no time. I'm out of time.

"I haven't lived." The words are ash in my mouth. I squeeze his wrists. "I wanted to be a mother."

"We have a beautiful girl. Her name is—?"

I'm momentarily lost, then I understand what he's doing. "Caroline. Her name is Caroline."

"She looks just like her momma. So beautiful. And so smart."

"She gets that from you."

The air is hazy with smoke. The airplane shivers in its death-spiral and part of me wonders how it doesn't tear itself to pieces. A battered man rolls down the aisle, clutching at the seats, and I can only watch it happen.

Fifty-two

"We have a boy." I lick my dry lips. "Caroline needs a brother."

"Noah."

I nod enthusiastically. "He takes after his daddy."

"You want Caroline to be an artist like you, but she's stubborn." He laughs, then grimaces. "She likes your piano instead."

"She can have all the piano lessons she wants. But if Noah wants to play football, I forbid it."

Forty-four

The plane convulses and luggage rains down from the overhead bins. A screaming woman tumbles down the aisle and Daniel pulls my gaze back to his.

"Noah can play baseball," he says.

"Baseball," I repeat woodenly. "Remember when he . . . ?" I don't know much about baseball and I falter.

"Hit a grand slam." Daniel's eyes are wet, his pupils large. "I was so proud."

"Caroline has a crush on a boy in her high school class."

"I forbid it!"

A choked laugh escapes my lips. "You can't stop true love. She's growing up."

"He's a good boy?"

"Reminds me of you." I cup Daniel's face.

Thirty-two

"Noah graduates second in his high school class."

"He's so disappointed he isn't first, but I can never be disappointed in him."

Daniels squeezes his eyes shut, a pained look on his face, then his brown eyes are drinking me in again. "Do you think he'll go to Columbia?"

"I think there's a certain girl he'd like to follow to Stanford."

"But Caroline is going to Juilliard."

"She has her heart set on it."

Twenty-four

"But look at you, the most famous sculptor in the world. Everyone wants a piece of you."

"They can't have me. I'm all yours."

"And since I've taken a job with that other law firm, I'm home all the time. But not so much that I annoy you."

"Never." The acrid air stings my nose, burns my eyes. "I'm too damn greedy. I want every second."

"You have it."

Nineteen

This eye in the center of the maelstrom where only we exist can't endure. I know our time is almost up and I come full circle, face-to-face with my mortality.

"I'm sorry I—"

Daniel puts his fingers to my lips. "Uh-uh. No regrets."

"Okay." I kiss his fingers. "No regrets."

"I've—" A trickle of blood slides out of the corner of his mouth. "I've never been more proud to be your husband." He touches my cheek.

Eleven

I know I'm loved. I can feel it. So strong. So palpable. That look in his eyes now, that look is everything. In this moment, it is everything and more. It is my universe.

Eight

He's crying now and that's when I lose it. Despite what I'd said earlier, I'm full of regret. "I didn't get enough time with you."

Six

"It's enough." That damn, beautiful sureness of his. Yes, it's enough. In a world so hateful, so ugly, it has to be enough.

Four

"Tell me something beautiful."

Three

The corners of his mouth pull up in a half-smile.

Two

He leans close, presses his lips to my ear . . .

One

And whispers my name.

Zero

Mike Akins got his start in writing by winning first place in the novel category for the 2001 Panhandle Professional Writers' Frontiers in Writing contest. Since then, he's been busy learning the craft, meeting great friends along the way. He loves giving back to the writing community and was the 2018 President of Texas High Plains Writers. He's currently on the executive committee of Amarillo ArtsFest, looking to promote Panhandle writers as part of an inaugural event showcasing the arts in Amarillo.

To Be a Man

A. C. Akins

Cody used to love his living room. He remodeled most of it himself. He scraped off the original floral wallpaper and painted it over with a welcoming pale green that his wife picked out. He spent more than a few tax returns on a canvas sectional and a leather recliner which he regularly polished and cleaned. On either side of the couch were wooden end tables which he built, sanded, and finished himself. The crown jewel was a sixty-inch flat screen emblazoned on the wall across from the sectional.

But he hated it now. Sitting on the sofa with his elbows propped on his knees, he stared at the only thing he hadn't fixed—the carpet. He'd meant to install hardwood flooring to make the room more modern, but never got around to it. Now he realized it soured the whole area. He sighed and reread the email on his phone as he took a sip of bourbon.

Cody's wife, Ellary, wandered in from the kitchen to find her husband on the couch. She wore a blue floral sundress that stopped just above her knees, her light brown hair pulled up in a messy bun. In her ears were the half carat diamond earrings Cody had bought her for their anniversary two years ago. She sat down on the other side of the sectional. "How did the interview go?"

He slid his phone into his pocket. "You look beautiful."

She scoffed. "I barely had time to do my hair this morning."

"It looks nice."

She leaned her back against the cushion and stretched her legs out over the chaise. "The interview?"

He took another sip. "It went okay, I guess."

"What did they say?"

He clasped the bourbon with both hands and stared down at the carpet again. "I was hoping to get the kids together before I said anything."

"Sarah is upstairs, and Timothy is with my mom. He should be home soon."

"I can get Sarah if you'd like."

She craned her head around to the staircase behind her. "Sarah!"

"You don't have to shout." He set his bourbon on the end table, then slowly trudged up the stairs and turned the corner down the hall.

He knocked on his daughter's partially open door, pushing it further with his knuckles. The lights were off in her room save for a dim orange glow from the lamp on her nightstand. The curtains were drawn over the window which composed much of the north wall. It was dark, even for dusk. She was lying in bed on her stomach, her phone casting bright blue light onto her face. He looked at the things he had bought for her—the phone, the queen sized mattress, the violin and music stand across the room. He felt a brief flash of pride for the life he had given her.

"Your mom and I need you downstairs," he said.

"One second," she answered, barely glancing up from her smartphone. He wanted to chastise her for blowing him off but couldn't. He lingered in the doorway watching his daughter's life play out in front of him. The entirety of her world existed between the few inches from her face to her phone.

Ellary was still sitting on the couch when Cody returned. She looked relaxed, her legs crossed over each other. Sarah sauntered down shortly after, sat down in the leather recliner, and immediately returned to her phone. The doorbell rang.

"Timothy is here," Ellary said and left to go answer the door.

Once she was gone, Sarah looked up from her phone. "Is everything okay?" she asked her father.

He let out a sigh and took a sip of bourbon. "I think so."

That was enough for her to continue scrolling. After a few minutes, Ellary returned with their six-year-old son.

"How was Grandma?" Cody asked.

"We went to the museum, and I got to see a big plane like the ones you worked on," his son replied.

Cody smiled. "Is that so?"

"What is this about?" Sarah asked.

Ellary sat back down on the sofa and Timothy next to her. "Don't look at me," she said.

Cody looked over at his young son beaming up at him. He'd not known how to be a role model before Timothy. Sarah had gravitated towards her mother ever since she was born. Once he had a son, he found himself watching how he treated Ellary and Sarah, how he handled the bills and carried himself at work. There was so much he wished he could take back, and he wondered if Timothy had watched him during those times. He was watching now.

"The plant emailed me today." He paused for a second and looked around at his family and at his home. At the dingy carpet and the repainted walls. At his beautiful wife and daughter and his handsome young son. At all of things he had bought and made for them. "I got the job," he finally said.

Ellary exhaled in relief but did not smile.

"Starting Monday, I'll be managing the plant."

"Does that mean you'll be the boss?" Timothy asked.

"Something like that," Cody said.

"I'm proud of you, Dad," Sarah said with a smile.

The family celebrated over dinner. Ellary made lasagna and they later watched a movie on the flat screen. Afterwards, Ellary took Timothy to bed despite his screaming protests, leaving Cody alone in the living room with his daughter. She was on her phone for most of the movie, but she had put it away now.

"Dad?" she started. "You don't have to say yes—I know money is tight—but," she paused. "I was thinking I could get a new violin?"

He remembered how she'd smiled when he bought her the first one. He hadn't expected her to keep with it, but four years and eight recitals later, violin had become Sarah's greatest devotion. He wanted nothing more than to see her smile like that again.

"The pegs are broken," she said, noticing his silence. "It doesn't stay tuned for long and—"

"Sure," he said, and immediately wished he hadn't.

Her face lit up in a smile. "Thank you so much!" She hugged her father tightly.

After he finished his bourbon and Sarah had retreated upstairs, Cody retired to the bedroom where Ellary was reading. Ellary often read mystery thrillers while Cody would sift through news articles on his phone. Occasionally they would kiss for a few minutes, and even more rarely they would fool around. Cody slid under the comforter and sunk his head into his pillow, staring at the ceiling. He turned toward his wife and began to brush her hair with his fingers. He removed her reading glasses and set them on the nightstand. He kissed her, and in a moment was straddling her and moved to kissing her neck. She seemed stiff and unresponsive.

"Do you want to stop?" Cody asked.

"No, no," she said. "I don't know."

Cody turned onto his side and propped himself up by his elbow. "Is something wrong? You've been distant all evening."

"I'm fine."

"You haven't smiled all night. Did I do something?" he asked.

"No, it's not that."

He kissed her cheek. "I know things haven't been good."

"Everything is fine," she said.

He ran his fingers through her hair again. "You can talk to me."

She stared down at her hands which she awkwardly folded in her lap. "God, Cody, can you just drop it?"

"Tell me what's wrong," he said, placing his hand on her shoulder.

"I had sex with someone else."

It was quiet in the bedroom. The TV was off and the kids were asleep. The slightest creak of the bed springs would've filled the room, but Cody didn't move. Only his chest rose steadily with his breath.

"You haven't worked in six months. You haven't... touched me in weeks."

He wanted to yell, scream, ball up his fist and demolish the wall above the headboard. But he was frozen. He looked at his wife, tears now in her eyes as she braced for his response, but he couldn't say anything. After a few minutes he got up, slipped on his boots, and zipped up his work jacket.

"Where are you going?" she asked.

"I need to think," he said.

Ellary buried her face into her pillow.

On his way down the hall, Cody peeked into his son's room. Timothy was sound asleep, his head turned slightly to the side allowing drool to spill onto the pillow. Everything would change when his son woke up. He couldn't give Timthoy the life he wanted. He couldn't get him a fancy watch or phone, no expensive tennis shoes or computers. But Cody's most crushing failure was how he'd robbed his son of a proper father. He wanted with everything in him to never have to tell his family who he was.

He stared once again at the carpet as he returned to the living room, finally accepting that he could never replace it now. The whole house felt incomplete and unfinished. He used to feel accomplished at the progress he made with the remodel, but now he could only think about the old floors, unpainted walls, and outdated appliances.

Cody walked outside and started down the sidewalk, lighting a cigarette as he went. He'd quit once, when Timothy was born, but he was always too weak to follow through. The rain had slowed to a drizzle. Over the sound of his boots softly scraping the concrete, he could faintly hear a violin coming from the window on the second story. It was effortless and beautiful, but the music stopped as she tuned a string. Cody hated himself more each time it did.

Ellary laid crying into her pillow. She'd sent Cody several texts but he hadn't responded. He was gone. After her sobbing slowed to a stop, she realized she could track her husband's phone from his computer. Desperate to know where he'd gone, she quietly snuck downstairs to the desktop and logged in. Open on the screen was Cody's email message from the plant.

We regret to inform you that the position you have applied for has already been filled. Thank you for your application, it said.

Hamsters Fly the American Way

Laura Harrison

I was going home. I had gone off to college, graduated, married, and divorced in the space of 8 years. What's worse, I had also quit my job. I was going home. That was all that was important to me now. Mom had flown to Austin to help me pack. The movers would load up the heavy furniture and drive the five hundred miles to Amarillo.

As soon as I had moved out of my house seven months ago, I had bought 3 hamsters: Friend, Freedom, Coco. A fourth, Coco Jr., was a later addition to the family. For four and a half years, I had begged to have a hamster, but my husband had forbidden me to have any pets other than the 2 dogs we shared. He now had custody of the dogs, but I would get them back. Mom and I packed all day. The driver I had hired to drive my U-Haul wanted to pick up the truck by evening. By six, we were done packing. Mom and I would fly to Amarillo in the morning.

"What are you going to do with the hamsters?" asked Mom. "Aren't you going to put them in the U-Haul?"

"No," I replied. "The number one killer of hamsters is a draft and I'm sure the driver will want the air conditioner on."

"Well then, what are you going to do?"

"We'll put the cages in the U-Haul and carry the hamsters in their balls and the little carry-on bag Lisa lent me. When we get to the airport, I'll put Coco and Coco Jr. in my pockets and you put Friend and Freedom in yours."

Mom had to ask one more question. "Are you allowed to have hamsters on the plane?"

"I don't know, but I don't need to worry about that right now," I replied.

"You'll have to figure something else out, because I'm not putting any hamsters in my pockets," Mom said stubbornly.

The driver arrived later that day and took off with the truck containing all my furniture and the four hamsters' cages. Mom and I slept in my vacant apartment on the floor with four hamsters running all night long in their hamster balls.

We had a flight out of Austin to Dallas (they tell me you have to stop in Dallas to get to heaven, too) and then from Dallas to Amarillo. My best friend Gayle would drive us to the airport and then keep the car until I sold it or donated it to charity. In the five years of being married, it had never occurred to Kevin my husband to buy me a new car. The car salesman had offered me two hundred and fifty dollars for it, but I had walked away disgusted and had decided to keep it until it cost more to fix it than to buy a new one.

Gayle drove us to the airport. I asked Mom again to go through with "The Plan."

"I don't think so," Mom said.

We got to the ticket counter and answered the two questions they always asked: had the luggage been in our immediate possession at all times and had any stranger given us anything to carry on board.

So far so good. Now all we have to do is get through security. Mom had made it quite clear she wasn't going to participate in "The Plan." I really had no option. There was no way I could stuff all four of them in my own pockets because Coco would probably mate with one, or Friend and Freedom would fight. When it was time, I handed the bag containing all the hamsters in their individual compartments to the agent standing behind the counter. I thought the x-rays might not be good for their health. The red-vested agent looked at my hamsters and asked, "Which airline will you be taking?"

"Southwest," I told her.

"Sorry ma'am, but there is a no pet policy on Southwest," she replied.

In utter frustration, I picked up the hamster balls and tried to get Mom's attention; she had already gone through security.

"They won't let me take them!" I yelled. "Go get your boarding pass and I'll let you know what I'm going to do."

After checking with American Airlines and having a ridiculous cost of $469 dollars quoted, I was really frustrated. Think, I told myself, I can do this! I thrive on crisis situations.

"Come on," I said to Gayle, who had not left yet. I had a Plan B. Gayle followed at my heels. We ran into the ladies restroom where I began to fill two of my pockets with Coco and Coco Jr. (Coco Jr. was the product of Coco and Friend being put in the same cage.) Gayle tried to put Freedom and Friend into her pockets. Finding it difficult to fit them into her jeans pockets, Gayle lifted her shirt and tucked them in it. The hamsters were now crawling inside her shirt. Gayle quickly decided this was not a good idea either. She began to move around spastically and it looked like she was dancing the "washing machine." After laughing at her for a minute, I told her sternly, "Stop that, now!" She stopped dancing and we walked out of the restroom side by side disposing of the carry-on in the trash can. My sister Lisa had lent me the carry-on (she had birds). I would have to buy her a new one.

Together we walked to another security check at the Austin Airport. I was going to try again. Another red-vested but buxom agent greeted us at the security point. "What are those?" she asked, "hamster balls?"

"Yes," I replied as I hurried through the people scanner. Gayle followed close behind me. "We made it!" I said happily. We ran around the corner and stuffed each hamster back into its ball. Now I had to get my boarding pass.

"Go on ahead and make sure Mom doesn't say anything," I ordered as we made our way to the gate. Before we could get there, however; Mom had jumped to her feet, clapped her hands, and exclaimed, "Jana, how did you do it!"

"Shhh!" I whispered in frustration. "I need to check in. You wait here with Gayle."

The agent behind the counter gave us a mean stare and demanded, "Where are they?" It was then I saw my mother talking with an agent on the other side. I glared at her. Thanks a lot Mom, I thought. My plan hadn't worked out after all. I stood there stunned. Mistaking my brief moment of thinking for defiance she said, "I'm going to call Security."

I yelled back at her, "You don't need to do that, because I'm not going." I turned my back and walked away.

Mom was forced to board the plane alone and tell Dad and Lisa what had happened. They would be disappointed, but I couldn't come home without my babies.

I spent the night at Gayle's house and came up with a new plan. The next morning I embarked on Plan C. I would drive to Dallas, leave my car with my brother Joe (who lives in Plano) and fly to Amarillo on American the next morning. He confirmed that pets were allowed on this airline.

The next day, I boldly approached the ticket agent and I plunked Freedom onto the counter. The woman glanced at the hamster and said, "That will be an additional fifty dollars." I felt silly paying fifty dollars for a four dollar pet. But I paid the agent and went in search of the gate. I boarded the plane and flew to Amarillo.

When I got to Amarillo, my sister greeted me happily. "Oh, Jana I'm so glad you finally made it. The mover had already arrived and the U-Haul was waiting for me at my parent's house. I would have to go house hunting when I got myself settled. But first a nap.

Two weeks later, Lisa met Kevin in Childress to pick up the dogs. He was living in an apartment now and they didn't allow dogs.

As I recounted the story to Lisa later that day, I told her, "The next time I fly I'm going with American Airlines."

Reining in a Dream

Lynnette Jalufka

Today, I am putting my dream into motion. After five years without horses, I bought the perfect horse: a black and white registered American Paint Horse named Colonel Peppy Kolache.

"His name doesn't make sense," my non-horse husband informs me.

So once again, I explain that a registered name is not supposed to make sense. It usually contains words about the horse's pedigree, along with the breeder's own inventions. In the case of this gelding, his name indicates he's descended from Colonels Smoking Gun, a champion paint reining horse. He's also related to a famous line of cow horses bred at the King Ranch in Texas. Plus, the breeder must love eating the sweet buns filled with fruit known as kolaches, as do I. The only name that matters is the "barn name," the name used every day. I decide to call him Kole.

I plan to use Kole in an upcoming breed show. I'm excited about showing again, though it's been ten years since I last stepped into a showring. And that had been a small local one. This is a major step up, but it's my dream to compete at such a level. Since Kole has had experience with that type of competition, we should make a good team.

We'll be competing in an event called reining, one of the most difficult western events. It combines speed and control. Different patterns call for various maneuvers, including 360-degree spins in place, 180-degree turnarounds called rollbacks, along with backing up. There are also large, fast circles and small, slow circles. Lead changes alter direction at a gallop. The sliding stops highlight the performance.

A horse slides on its hind hooves while stopping from a gallop. All the while, I must constantly use my entire body to tell the horse what to do when. It's a complicated dance between horse and rider to make the four-minute ride appear effortless.

Kole and I have 120 days to master all the steps before showtime.

One hundred and thirteen days to go. We've completed our first week getting to know each another. I've discovered Kole loves to raise his upper lip in the horse equivalent of a smile when he wants treats. He's hard to resist when he's so cute.

One hundred and ten days to go. I hate circles. Why did I pick an event that required circles? Galloping a horse in a perfectly round shape is not as easy as it seems. It takes coordination from my entire body. Today, our circles turned into eggs. Time to go back to the basics. So, I set orange cones in a circle. We spent several minutes going around them at different speeds.

One hundred days to go. Kole gets his new sliding shoes on his hind hooves today. Husband rolls his eyes at the cost. He does the same thing when I remind him Kole needs them every six weeks.

Eighty-five days to go. The first rule of reining is "Count the spins. Count the spins. Count the spins." Most patterns call for spins in groups of four. I sit on Kole, drumming my fingers on the saddle horn, wondering whether we did three, four, or five. One under or over means disqualification. I focus on the cone next to the fence in the arena and count it as we spin again. This time, I know we did four.

Sixty days to go. We take a break from training to go on a trail ride with friends. Surrounded by nature's beauty, I relax. That is, until a horse throws a friend and heads back down the trail by itself. Kole's speed comes in handy as we pursue it. I finally grab the horse's reins when it stops to graze.

Thirty days to go. I'm on the phone with Mom discussing my show outfit: western hat, belt, jeans, shirt, and boots. When I showed horses in 4-H, we had a deal. I would take care of the horse while she would take care of me. Now, I'm doing it all by myself, though

Husband is trying to be helpful. "You look beautiful," he says at whatever I model for him.

Fifteen days to go. Kole has forgotten he is a reining horse. His maneuvers are sloppy. My cues are off. I put my head down on the kitchen table and choke back the tears. Am I good enough for this show, or am I just kidding myself? Husband gives me a hug. "You'll do better next time," he says. "Don't give up. You've worked so hard." It's enough to make me try again tomorrow.

Fourteen days to go. Kole and I are a dynamite team. If we perform like this at the show, we have a great chance of winning.

Five days to go. I polish my saddle and bridle. The engraving on a western saddle looks exquisite, but it's a pain to clean those tiny crevices with an old toothbrush. At least, the saddle oil softens my hands.

Four days to go. I clip the long hairs on Kole's legs. After concentrating on a hind hoof, I glance up at the muscles in his hindquarters. I'm amazed at how large this thousand-pound animal is! Kole could easily crush me if he wanted to, but he stands patiently, swishing his tail at a fly.

One day to go. I should wear a swimsuit when I give a horse a bath. I always end up soaked. Kole is no help. He tries to bite the end of the water hose, spraying water on me when he succeeds. After drying him off, I put a horse sheet on him, so he won't get dirty. Husband helps me pack the truck and trailer. We load Kole, then drive two hundred miles to the showgrounds. By the time I get Kole settled in his stall and checked into the hotel, it's 10 p.m. I'm exhausted.

Showtime. I head to the showgrounds at 5 a.m. to feed Kole. He gives me a big smile as if this was just an ordinary day. I spend the morning hours watching my fellow competitors perform in different events. They are younger than me and much more experienced. Butterflies take flight in my stomach. Am I ready for this? I remind myself that I have worked just as hard as my competition. I must remain calm for Kole's sake.

As my class nears, I dress in my show outfit and saddle Kole. We go through our usual warm-up routine in the designated arena, then wait. And wait. My class is next.

Husband wishes me luck. "I'm proud of you," he says, giving me a kiss. He leaves to find the perfect spot to video the performance.

"Number 283, you're up," the gate keeper calls. "Three ninety-one, you're next. Three fifteen, be thinking about it."

We're 315. I ride over to the entrance of the main arena. "We can do this, boy," I say as I pet Kole's neck. I go over the pattern in my mind for the hundredth time.

"Number 315, you're up."

I take a deep breath, then kick Kole into a gallop. We thunder down the length of the main arena. I wait until I see the last marker before cueing our first stop. Kole slides beautifully. We go into a left rollback and charge back down the arena to the opposite side for another sliding stop. After a rollback to the right, we gallop again. This time, we slide in the center of the arena. We back up to the center marker and hesitate. Time to catch my breath.

"Count the spins," I remind myself as I give the cue. Kole turns to the right at a dizzying pace, each one faster than the one before. I count the center marker. One, two, three, whoa! We repeat going to the left. I'm thankful for another hesitation to clear my head.

Kole slowly starts our right circles. I use my legs and body to keep him at a gallop. We finish two at speed then slow down for a smaller circle. At the center of the arena, we change leads to perform our circles to the left. I urge Kole to keep his speed as if we were racing in the Kentucky Derby. After completing two, we slow to a pace in our small circle that would make the horses in the western pleasure class envious.

We change leads again and gallop around the end of the arena. Kole gives me one more burst of speed. We finish our pattern with a nice sliding stop.

I pet Kole's neck as we exit the arena, feeling hot sweat beneath my hand. He's breathing hard. So am I. I'm completely drained. As far as I could tell, we didn't make any big errors. I'm happy. It doesn't matter what the judges think. We did our best, and that's all that counts.

Husband joins me back in the warm-up arena. "You were great," he says, like he knows how to judge reining. I appreciate the compliment anyway. Kole rubs his wet head on Husband's shirt. Husband smiles.

The announcer calls the placings for my class. I hope for a ribbon. "In third place, number 315, Colonel Peppy Kolache." I jump off Kole, hug his neck, and run to collect my white ribbon. I proudly wave it as I carry it back.

Husband hugs me, though I'm covered in sweat. "I'm proud of you," he says. "You worked hard for this."

I have reason to be proud. I proved I could compete at a large breed show after a long absence from showing. Kole made my dream a reality.

We walk back to the barn, where Kole gets a shower along with handfuls of carrots. And I start planning for the next show.

Three Poems

Juliana Lightle

Blood Quantum

This poem is dedicated to Sherman Alexie whose poem, "13/16" begins with: "I cut my self into sixteen equal pieces…"

My grandson cuts himself into 16 equal pieces:

4/16 Urhobo from Africa
3/16 Spanish from Spain
4/16 other European—two Swiss
       German great great-grandfathers
       (Werth and Kaiser), Irish, English
       and who knows what
3/16 Mexican—whatever mixtures that may be
2/16 Navaho

Who am I? What am I?
Who are you? What are you?
Do we really know?
Who sets the rules?
       white men
       black
       Indian
       Native American
       Irish

English
German
from where and for whom?

He looks Navaho:
-blue black straight hair,
-pale brown skin,
-obsidian eyes.
One four-year-old girl asks him,
"Are you an American Indian?"
His six your old self says nothing.
She repeats,
"Are you an American Indian?"
He says, "It's complicated."

The Navaho won't claim him, too little blood.
He needs ¼ , not 1/8.
Caddo and Fort Sill Apache allow 1/16, not Navahos.
¼ blood is for
-Sioux
-Cheyenne
-Kiowa
-Navaho
1/8 works for Comanche and Pawnee.
Some Cherokees only want a Cherokee ancestor.

But he is none of those.
Is he Navaho?
Is he white?
The Old South goes by the one drop rule:
one drop of Negro…
Is a person with 99/100 percent white
and 1/100 black , black?
Who says?
Kids at school ask, What are you?"

He tells them.
They say, "You're lying!"

I only know specifically about two ancestors,
       the Swiss Germans.
Another great grandfather disappeared during the Civil War.
I don't even know his name.
Who am I?
Who are you?
I think I'll get a DNA test.
Then I'll know how many pieces I need to cut myself into.

STAR

The phone rings.
"Star's dead. There's blood everywhere.
He's hanging from the gate by one hoof.
Blood is all over Rosie's face.
It's dreadful."
A tear choked voice.
"You can't bring D'mitri home."
D'mitri's nine. Star belongs to him.
Shock, tears, disbelief.
Last night Star ran, bucked, reared,
chased around, playing.
How?
The pen's all pipe, no sharp edges,
nothing harmful, consistently inspected.

D'mitri goes home with me. He says,
"Nana, I have to see him;
I have to know what happened."
Slowly, in dread, we walk behind the barn.
Star's hanging by one hoof in the three inch
space between the gate and fence,
ankle broken.
The blood covered fence, gate, and ground
stare at me.
It's hot, his body's stiff.
He must be moved.
Coyotes will come in the night,
drawn by the smell of blood, of death.
The neighbor brings his big red tractor;
a winch pulls Star's young body free,
gently lays him on the cold, grey,
cement barn floor.
His shining copper coat no longer shines.

D'mitri and I remember bottle feeding him
after Miracle died, teaching him to lead.
We stare at Star's body in disbelief.
Kindly, the neighbor says,
"He died quick, femoral artery cut by bone,
bled out."

For hours, Rosie and Cool stand at the spot
where Star died.
They do not even leave to eat alfalfa.
It takes me hours to wash away the blood.
It takes D'mitri ten months to go back to the barn,
to ride Rosie again.

The Farrier

He looks like the typical cowboy
with no cowboy hat.
A cowboy hat would get in the way
up against a horse.
Pale blue eyes,
grey, handlebar moustache,
pack of Camels,
Australian shepherd, Chili, by his side.
After the trimming
he sits and talks to me
for two hours.
He tells me a story
he told me last time.
I listen as if it were the first time.

People call him from Oklahoma City.
They want a shoer.
He tells them,
*"Too far unless
there's ten horses at 85 a head."*
They agree.
He gets there with Chili,
a pup then.
He starts to tie her up.
*"No need;
let her play with our puppy."*
He does.
They invite him out.
It's New Year's Eve.

*"The dive they took me to
was real rough, real rough,*

so rough I'd worry about
my safety even with two 45s.
Next morning I'm ready
for the other six horses.
There are none."
He packs up,
comes home.
Chili won't eat,
won't play.
It's parvo.
She's had the vaccine
but not enough time.
"The people in Oklahoma City
lied about the horses
about the parvo.
Chili stayed on IVs for five days."

Today, Chili's a dog dynamo,
grown with puppy energy.
She and Isabella play.
He says,
"You must be rich to build this place."
I laugh.
"Rich, I'm not rich.
Lucky maybe,
no, not lucky.
I don't believe in luck."

A person makes her own luck.
Smart helps, sometimes.

Raised on a family farm in northwester Missouri, Juliana Lightle, became a singer, college administrator, corporate manager and consultant, race horse breeder, educator, and author. Her previous publications include Sexual Harassment in the Work Place: A Guide to Prevention, On the Rim of Wonder, *a memoir in poetry, as well as articles in newspapers and journals. Her new book,* You're Gonna Eat That?!—Adventures with Food, Family, and Friends, *will be published in early 2019. A former board member of the Story Circle Network, an organization devoted to promoting women's stories, she currently teaches English and Spanish in the Panhandle of Texas.*

Jesus the Offering for Sin

James D. Quiggle

An offering for sin must be made physically as well as spiritually. The body as well as the soul must suffer the penalty, because the penalty for sin is physical and spiritual. When Adam and Eve sinned they were separated from fellowship with God: a spiritual death. Physically, they continued their slow decline to an inevitable physical death, Genesis 3:19 (there is nothing to suggest they were created physically immortal). So too their children, as revealed in the repeated "and he died" in Genesis 5, and throughout Scripture as men, women, and children physically died.

Physical death is the separation of the soul from the body. The spiritual death of the unsaved soul is separation from a relationship with God. "Your sins have separated you from your God; your sins have hidden your God from you so that he will not hear you," Isaiah 59:2. "The person who sins shall die," Ezekiel 18:20. Paul said to the Ephesians that they had at one time been "dead in trespasses and sins," 2:1, 5, indicating spiritual death; and then they had been made "alive together with Christ," 2:5, indicating salvation and spiritual life. Sin causes physical and spiritual death.

To fully propitiate God for sin requires both physical and spiritual deaths. The Old Testament animal sacrifices represented the physical death of the believer, and so were limited. Jesus made the necessary physical and spiritual deaths in his propitiation for sin.

Jesus Died Physically

Skeptics doubt Jesus' physical death, stating that he merely fainted on the cross and revived in the coolness of the tomb. Such opinions show a gross ignorance of the facts.

The Roman soldiers were masters of death. As in any military unit they had dealt death on the battlefield—not long distance as is done today, but face to face with a sword or spear. Each member of the Jerusalem unit was experienced at recognizing death. As in any military unit the crucifixion detail would have been a rotating duty performed by every member of the unit, so each was experienced at recognizing death by crucifixion. One of the soldiers, seeing that Jesus was dead, John 19:33 (compare Matthew 27:54; Mark 15:44–45; Luke 23:47), stabbed the body through the heart with a spear. Why did he do this if he knew Jesus was dead? In the Roman military the soldiers responsible for the execution would suffer the penalty of the condemned if they allowed the condemned to escape. The soldier wanted to make sure there was no mistake. Out of a strong sense of self-preservation he stabbed Jesus through the heart to make sure his initial evaluation was correct: Jesus was dead.

Jesus' state of death was confirmed to Pilate by the Centurion in charge, Mark 15:44. Not merely that Jesus was dead, but that "he had been dead for some time." The recognition of his death, the assurance of his death, the passing of time from his death, and stabbing Jesus in the heart after his death assured the Roman Centurion and Pilate that Jesus had died. They knew their business better than skeptics and critics.

Jesus' enemies also knew he was dead. In the ancient world people died at home, in the streets, on the battlefield, and at places of execution. Everyone from childhood to old age knew and recognized the state of death, for they saw death face to face in their daily experiences. Jesus' enemies went to Pilate to ask for guards for the tomb, saying, Matthew 27:63, "we remember while he was still alive," indicating their knowledge that Jesus was dead. They had watched him die on the cross. They had seen the soldier stab Jesus through the heart. They asked Pilate for guards to prevent Jesus' disciples from stealing his dead body, thereby claiming a resurrection from the dead. Never mind that Jesus' followers were too frightened, discouraged, and disorganized to steal the body. The chief priests and

Pharisees knew Jesus was dead and wanted everyone to remember him as he was: physically dead.

The tomb was closed, the entrance was blocked by a large stone, and the tomb was guarded by Roman soldiers, Matthew 28:65–66. Jesus resurrected and left without their knowledge. Angels came and rolled the stone away from the tomb; the soldiers trembled for fear and became comatose because of their fright. When they had recovered, they knew what would happen to them should it be reported to Pilate that Jesus' body was missing from the tomb: they would be executed. So they told the priests, who guaranteed their security should Pilate hear of this, and took money to lie about Jesus.

Jesus' dead body was wrapped in linen cloth, spices, and aromatic gums, Matthew 27:59; Mark 15:46; Luke 23:53. John 19:39–40 says he was wrapped in strips of linen cloth with about seventy-five pounds (100 *litras*) of myrrh and aloes, with spices. He wasn't wrapped in a shroud, he was wrapped in strips of cloth "as the custom of the Jews is to bury" (NKJV). Myrrh was an exuded gum from a tree which could be dried to a solid resin and, among other uses, was used for embalming. The body was wrapped in multiple layers of linen strips of cloth. Each layer was coated with the myrrh, aloes, and spices. As these dried the cloth was hardened by the dried resin of the myrrh. No one so embalmed could have wriggled out of the hardened cloths, compare John 11:44. The resurrected Jesus rose out of the cloths without disturbing them, John 20:6, in the same manner as he suddenly appeared in the upper room, John 20:19, 26, the doors being shut.

Consider the testimony of the two men who embalmed Jesus. Nicodemus and Joseph knew Jesus was dead, John 19:38–42. Death was a constant presence in the ancient world. There were no hospices, no hospitals, no funeral homes, no cremation societies. Family, relatives, and friends buried their dead. They knew a dead body when they saw one. Jesus died about 3:00 p.m. Sunset was about 6:00 p.m. Washing the body (the Jewish custom) and then embalming the body with layer upon layer of linen strips and myrrh and aloes and spices would have taken more than an hour. If Jesus had merely fainted, then the constant handling required to wash and wrap the body would have revived him. Jesus was physically dead. The soldiers knew he was dead, his enemies knew he was dead, and his friends knew he was dead.

Scripture states the death of Jesus in the plainest terms. Matthew 27:50, Jesus yielded up his spirit. Mark 15:37, Jesus breathed his last. Luke 23:46, Jesus breathed his last. John 19:30, Jesus gave up his spirit. He died physically, fully satisfying the physical penalty for sin.

Jesus Died Spiritually

Someone might question whether Jesus died from the physical stress of the crucifixion, or deliberately and voluntarily died to pay the penalty for sin. Jesus is the offering and the offeror: in the Old Testament type the offeror killed the sin offering, Leviticus 4:4, 24, 29, 33. John 19:30 answers the question. "Jesus said, 'It is finished.' Then bowing his head he gave up his spirit." Jesus held up his head during the crucifixion, until the spiritual payment of the penalty was completed. He declared his work was finished, then he deliberately and purposefully separated his soul from his body: he voluntarily caused his physical death (the offeror killed the sacrifice). The word translated "it is finished," is *teléō*, "to complete something, not merely to end it, but to bring it to perfection or its destined goal." Before he died physically Jesus cried out, *"Tetelestai,"* the perfect tense of the verb *teléō*, indicating the action of the verb was brought to completion. It was his cry of victory at having completed the propitiation for sin, both the spiritual death now past, and the physical death about to come.

Jesus must have completed the spiritual death for sin before he caused his physical death. Spiritual death is separation from God. Was Jesus spiritually separated from God while on the cross? Yes, seen at Mark 15:34 when he said, *"Eloi, eloi, lama sabachthani,"* which being translated is, "My God, my God, why have you forsaken me?" These were not the words of a man caught unaware by his spiritual separation from the Father. These were not the words of a man surprised by impending physical death. This was an exclamation made for our sakes, so we would know Jesus suffered and died spiritually.

Jesus knew he would suffer separation from God the Father when he became sin for us. In the Garden he prayed that "this cup" might pass from him. He was not praying about physical death. He had become incarnate to seek and save that which was lost, Matthew 18:11; Luke 19:10, so he knew he would die physically as part of the penalty for sin. He had, Luke 12:50, a "baptism to be baptized with," and was "distressed until it is accomplished," referring to his suffering on the cross both spiritually and physically.

Moreover, Jesus knew he would make it through physical and spiritual death without lasting harm. He told the repentant thief on the cross that he would be with him in heaven that very day. His good news for the thief indicated Jesus knew the spiritual and physical penalties for sin were about to be paid in full.

As his time of spiritual death was ending, and the time for his physical death drew near, he was thirsty. He knew every Scripture from his incarnation to this moment had been fulfilled, except one, Psalm 69:21, "for my thirst they gave me vinegar to drink." He said "I thirst," John 19:28; and then he drank, John 19:30a; he gave his cry of victory, Mark 15:34; and then he bowed his head and separated his soul from his body, John 19:30b. Before he died physically Jesus knew he had accomplished the spiritual death required by the penalty for sin.

The cry "My God, my God why have your forsaken me" came at the end of three hours of darkness, Mark 15:33–34. Before that last three hours on the cross he had asked the Father to forgive his executioners. He had saved the repentant thief. He had given his mother into the protective care of his disciple John (who took her away before the darkness began, John 19:27). Then, beginning about noon (Matthew 27:45), darkness covered the whole land for three hours. God was transacting business with the God-man. The Trinity had imputed sin to Jesus the Christ. He was suffering the undiluted wrath of God against sin. God covered the moment in darkness, to give his Son dignity in his sufferings, and to reveal the spiritual darkness of the moment when the Creator suffered for his sinful creature.

Because Jesus suffered for the judicial guilt of sin, not the moral defilement of sin, the Trinity did not separate from God the Son—an impossibility since they are the same essence. What took place was God separating from fellowship with the God-man. Isaiah 59:2, "Your sins have separated you from your God; your sins have hidden your God from you so that he will not hear you." The hours of darkness were when Christ suffered a temporary, but altogether genuine, spiritual death: separation from God because he "became sin for us."

His entire life Jesus had experienced fellowship with God, an unbroken and intimate communion. When he imputed man's sins to himself, that intimate communion the God-man had always had with the Father and Spirit was forsaken for three hours. That was the moment he dreaded, the moment he prayed about in the Garden of Gethsemane, that it might pass from him; but he submitted to God's will for the sake of sinners. Jesus the Christ took on the debt of sin; God turned his back to his son; Jesus suffered the spiritual death of separation from God.

During his last moments of physical life on the cross, we can see that the sin-debt was fully paid. Earlier he had cried out that God had forsaken him. Now he said, Luke 23:46, "Father." This word from their familial and filial relationship indicated the spiritual penalty had been paid and his fellowship with God had been restored. He said, "Father, into your hands I commit [entrust] my spirit," knowing that he would be received in heaven. And then he breathed his last. With the physical and spiritual penalties of sin paid in full, with every necessary Scripture fulfilled, he caused his soul to separate from his body, and went to his Father, taking the saved thief with him.

James D. Quiggle holds Master's degrees in religion and theology and has been teaching and writing about the Bible for over forty years. He is the author of over 40 published non-fiction works on the Bible.

Transformation

Elise Phillips

"We're going to have to talk about it sooner or later," Tom said from his spot at the kitchen table. A crossword puzzle sat before him, blank, waiting to be completed. It was his normal after dinner ritual and usually relaxed him. Tonight, it wasn't working. He twirled his pen from finger to finger as he watched his wife finish the supper dishes and tidy the kitchen. Although gray was starting to sneak into her auburn hair and wrinkles had settled around her eyes, she was still as beautiful to him as she had been the day they met. His eyes followed her through the kitchen as she cleaned the already spotless counters and spruced the pin neat room, each of her movements weighed down by tension and worry.

"Hon," he started, preparing to try again since she had failed to answer him.

"I heard you," Marie snapped. She wadded the cleaning rag into a wet ball and tossed it onto the counter, then turned to face him. She studied him a moment, noting the thinning white-blonde hair and the worry lines across his forehead. He was not the young man he once was, and he always carried a heavy burden in those gray blue eyes she loved so much. But tonight, he seemed to have aged years in the hours since dinner and that burden had doubled as the eyes watching her carried more worry than she had ever seen.

They were the only ones still up and about and could finally discuss the evening's events without interruption. The explosive dinner had ended hours ago. All of their girls, three teenage balls of hormones, had retreated to their bedrooms in a huff, each one angry and upset for very different reasons. As evening had turned to night the house had settled and gone quiet, lights slowly winking out as the girls had gone to bed. Marie and Tom had finally come together in the kitchen after busying themselves with meaningless tasks, each trying to process the news they'd received.

In the dark house, the day-time-bright kitchen was a cage—a prison—keeping them within the confines of its light, forcing them to come face to face with everything they'd been avoiding all evening. Yet still they stared at each other in silence. Around the room, the memories of the dinner fight echoed, bouncing around, refusing to go still. *You're what?! I could have told you she was sneaking out with Perry, but no one listens to me. Shut-up Julie! You shut up Laney! Girls!* Everyone had said things they shouldn't have. Julie and Amy shouldn't have even been part of the conversation, they were still so young. But Laney had planned it well, dropping the bomb with three simple words, *I'm pregnant y'all.* With the younger girls there, Tom and Marie had been forced to keep their questions unasked, internalized, eating them up from within their confused and hurting hearts. The younger girls didn't need to be a part of the conversations that would surely come soon. Laney and her parents had so much ground to cover. And so much to prepare for. Each one's world had changed at dinner. Even the younger girls. No one would be the same ever again.

Tom resumed twirling his pen as he watched her, his whole body sagging under the stressful thoughts that ran restlessly through his mind. In the harsh lights, Marie looked so much older. Had it really only been sixteen years of parenthood? Married at eighteen, parents before they both had reached twenty, life had gone by so quickly since Laney had joined the world. He was sure it had been longer since they'd welcomed their first born to the family. Most days it felt longer. Those naively happy teens they had been were far gone; it had to be longer than sixteen years.

From the back of the house, in the inky darkness, came the sound of a door slamming, then water running. "At least she's still here. At least she didn't take off," Marie finally spoke, staring toward the back of the house, thinking of their oldest daughter, picturing her going from her room to the bathroom. Laney was all long legs and long arms, built just like Marie. A tanned, lean girl on the edge of adulthood, yet she was still her baby. Even if she'd made a huge mistake, she was still her baby.

"I don't know what we're going to do, Marie."

"She's our daughter. We're going to stand by her and help her." Marie turned back to the half emptied sink and picked up the pan she'd left to soak. She stared at it as the soap and soggy bits of food slid down the surface, then placed it back into the water. "It is our job as parents. We will help her however we can."

Marie stared out into the night through the small window above the sink. The hours since dinner seemed like a dream. No, she corrected, a nightmare. She wondered what was out there in the darkness beyond the reach of the light cast by her window. Maybe it was where her normal life still existed. She wondered if all of this would fade away with the dawn and normalcy would return.

"What is my congregation going to say?" That was Tom's first and deepest fear. He voiced it almost involuntarily. He couldn't think of anything else until it was out in the open. "What will they say? What will they think when they find out? How can I lead a church when I can't control my own child? How can I preach about Christian values when my daughter is blatantly disobeying them?" He spoke the words in a rush, directing them down to the blank puzzle rather than his wife.

He looked up when he felt her stare. He met her anger with shame. He knew his first thoughts shouldn't be about his own problems. But he couldn't turn off those questions running through his mind.

"This isn't about you Tom." She sighed and walked over to join him at the table. "This isn't about either of us or our church. We'll worry about the congregation and everyone else later. Right now we need to focus on Laney. We need to guide her through this carefully."

"We could send her away. She could go live with my parents in Montana."

Marie was silent, instantly fuming at the idea of sending Laney away in shame. Her daughter would not be sent away, she was certain of that. Her hands, still red from the hot water, were knitted together so tight her knuckles were white. She stared at her husband, trying to hold on to her rising temper, wondering who this suddenly selfish man was. Where had her kind, caring Tom gone? Who was this man, this new version of her partner, who was so concerned what other people would think?

She opened her mouth to speak but quickly shut it when Laney drifted in from the darkened living room. Laney was in her pajamas and was free of her normal carefully applied makeup and perfectly styled hair. She looked so young in the pastel clothes and the simple ponytail that, for a moment, Marie thought everything had been a joke. And then Laney stood on tiptoe to reach for a box of cereal and her shirt rose, revealing her belly and the slight swelling from the child she carried. No, it had not been a joke. It was all very real. Marie felt foolish for not noticing how much her oldest had changed over the past several months.

Tom and Marie watched as Laney made a bowl of cereal and a poured a glass of juice. Their eyes followed her around the kitchen and then lost her in the darkness as she fled back to her bedroom. In unison they sighed and turned back to each other.

"We'll sit her down tomorrow and talk about this." Again it was Marie who broke the silence. Tom looked at her blankly; his mind still stuck on what people would say when the preacher at the biggest church in the city suddenly had a pregnant teen in his family.

"And that boy. He's part of this, too." She was a smart girl and he laid most of the blame for this on the rarely seen Perry, her boyfriend of three short months. "What if this costs me my church?"

Marie sighed again before responding. "Again Tom, this isn't about you. If the church can't look past a single lapse in judgment, then we shouldn't be a part of it anymore."

They slipped back into silence. From the back of the house, a door opened softly, someone clearly trying to go unnoticed. Laney's muffled voice came down the hallway toward them, too distant to be understood. Their middle child, Julie, spoke next, also just a whispered voice in the silent house. The youngest, Amy, would soon follow. The sisters gravitated toward each other in times of crisis. Tonight was no different. Marie pictured them each slipping down the hall to Laney's room and ending up crammed together in her bed. They would stay that way all night, talking, taking comfort in each other. They were such good girls.

"What if we get her an abortion?"

Marie's green eyes flashed with anger. She pointed across the table at Tom. "That is the last time you'll say that. An abortion is not, I repeat, not an option."

"I know." Tom hung his head, red-faced and ashamed. "I don't know where that came from."

They both dropped their eyes to the table, minds swimming with all the unasked questions. *How could they not have seen this coming? What had happened to their good, responsible daughter? Was the boyfriend really the problem or was it Laney?* They suddenly had a stranger living in their house.

Tom lifted his head, opening his mouth to speak, but Marie sensed his question and stopped him.

"I swear by all that is good and holy, Tom. If you ask one more self-centered question, I will leave you." She said the words with a hint of a smile. *By all that is good and holy*—it was her favorite expression. The familiar phrase was usually followed by the threat of an extreme action. It always made Tom smile, and tonight was no different.

Tom snapped his mouth shut and dropped his eyes to the crossword puzzle in front of him. He picked up his pen and resumed twirling it from finger to finger.

"What is a fourteen letter word meaning change?" It was a desperate move aimed at releasing the tension in the room. Six across had been the first question his eyes had landed on.

Marie thought a moment. "Transformation." If that wasn't a sign from God she didn't know what was. A feeling of comfort settled on her shoulders like a warm blanket. It was going to be a rough several months. Their whole world was going to have to be rebuilt. They might lose their church. They might have to move the whole family up to Montana. But they would weather the storm. She just knew it. Deep in her soul, she knew it.

From the back of the house a door slammed and the sound of retching echoed down the hallway. Tom and Marie locked eyes and Marie smiled.

"It will be okay." She pushed back her chair and walked to the fridge, repeating Laney's tiptoed reach into the cabinet above, pulling out a tin of crackers. She headed out of the room, pausing behind Tom's chair.

"It will be okay," she repeated. "He'll take care of us."

Tom glanced up to Heaven and then turned to watch his wife disappear down the dark hallway. Light flooded the space as she opened the door to the bathroom.

"Laney, honey."

"Oh, Momma."

She sounded so lost and Tom was reminded that, pregnant or not, she was still just a kid that needed her parents love and support. The door closed and the hall went dark again. Alone, Tom folded his hands and bowed his head, praying for God's guidance and help.

Praise Him and Dance

Jacie Sellars

Even though I'm only fourteen, it feels like I've always been a dancer. When I was three, I started taking ballet classes, and they became a constant in my life. Even though I grew up and went through many different seasons, I could always go to the dance studio. I would begin a class with pliés and tendus, and as I worked my way through every combination, I would be at peace and everything else would go away for a while. Ballet was hard, but I loved it. I had big dreams, and some of them came true, but things started to change when I was almost thirteen.

I walked into the studio at the beginning of my seventh-grade year excited for everything to start back up again. I saw some of my friends in the hallway chattering excitedly, and when I started listening carefully, I realized it was because they had all been moved to the advanced level. I hadn't been moved up, but I was happy for my friends and I thought they deserved it. I was a little disappointed, but I would be fine. I shoved my emotions down and danced, but that day was different because for the first time, I heard a voice in the back of my mind. **You are not good enough. You don't deserve anything.** This presence in my mind scared me. I went home and let myself cry, thinking that was the end of handling things immaturely, but it was only the beginning of my internal fight.

You just messed up. You're terrible at this. I tried to shake away the pessimistic thoughts in class a few days later as I went into my next pirouette, but I still fumbled and fell out of the turn. I told myself it was just an off day. **No it's not, you're just awful.** I tried to escape the horrible voice, but every time I pushed it away, it came back stronger. I felt determined to stay focused, but every slip up sent my mind spiraling into more negativity. It laughed when I got corrected. **Everyone knows you're just a fraud,** it said. **They can't believe you ever thought you could do this.** I tried to stay calm, but panic overtook me and I made even more mistakes.

I left that day feeling frustration and doubt where I had once felt happiness. I remembered discovering the magic of ballet after my very first recital. I'd wanted to keep dancing long after I left the auditorium. I had taken class after class, and when I was five I was able to join a Christian ballet studio that had a focus on using dance to worship. I loved dancing for Jesus, and I'd come to know Him as my Lord and Savior three years later when I was eight. It was the beginning of a golden era, but everything felt different now. What was wrong with me?

"So, the trip is during the dress rehearsal week?" I asked my mom in disbelief. She nodded sadly. I was immediately torn between the upcoming story ballet my studio had announced and a school trip I had looked forward to for years. I had been in a ballet before and I knew how amazing it was, but my school's seventh grade trip was to a charity in Arkansas. Students before me had told me it would change my life. I knew missing dress rehearsals was not usually accepted, so I would probably have to choose. **See, this is a sign you should just quit dancing.** Even though I tried so hard to ignore my traitorous thoughts, I had to admit it felt like the world was trying to pull me away from what I loved. My dreams were slipping through my fingers, and I didn't know how to hold on. I desperately prayed I could somehow do both.

"So Jacie, are you going to do basketball this year? We need someone your height on the team." I calmly told the curious girls from school I was sticking with ballet and tried to ignore their disappointment. I knew basketball was what girls who are six feet tall are "supposed to do," but it was never my thing. However, in dance class later that day, I began to feel unsure. **You're too tall to succeed at this. Tall dancers never make it.** Even though I'd always had supportive people around me, I had heard things like this my whole life in hushed whispers or conversations where people didn't seem to realize I was listening. I had always ignored these whispering voices etched into my subconscious, but now they seemed deafening. I suddenly had the most terrifying thought yet. **You don't belong here. You shouldn't be doing this.** I had spent the past few weeks being meticulous about my dancing and improving my technique in pursuit of my dreams, but that horrible conclusion that I didn't belong made me realize my dreams probably wouldn't happen. For the first time in almost ten years of ballet, I felt hopeless.

My hopelessness continued until October when a professional ballet company hosted a workshop over the weekend. They'd moved me to tears when they performed a ballet about Holocaust survivors. Learning from them in classical ballet, contemporary, conditioning, jazz and variations was amazing. I was actually able to start ignoring the voices inside my head for the first time in months. Now, I was at creative worship, and we danced our stories of salvation and attributes of God.

At the end, they played Christian songs and just let us dance however we wanted to. It was in this moment of free worship that I felt joy—pure, wonderful happiness, for the first time in a long time. I remembered why I loved ballet in the first place. During my childhood, every moment I had spent at my ballet studio and onstage felt like a fairytale. I was a shy kid, but when I began to dance I felt like I could truly express myself and worship through every plié, jump, and turn. I grew up, but the amazing feeling I got when I performed for Jesus stayed the same. That's when I decided I wasn't going to let my insecurities continue to steal my joy. I had tried to ignore my negative thoughts and focus on my ballet technique, but it wasn't working. I realized I would need to go to God if I wanted to solve my problems and reclaim my joy. I started to pray.

At first, talking to God was hard. I spilled out all my tumultuous emotions in prayer, and I felt angry at God. I asked Him why He put me in ballet if I couldn't have success in it or had the wrong body for it. I wondered how this could be a part of His plan. My inner voice egged on this idea. **You really aren't supposed to do this. God couldn't have put this in His plan for you. You're just going to fail.** In the end, I begged for answers, but I couldn't seem to hear any. I spent many nights on my knees in tears pleading with Him, and even though I didn't see God at work at first, things began to look up a bit. I found out I could participate in the story ballet and go on my school trip. I was also able to be in a Christmas show where I used my own choreography and felt happy with my performance. So that holiday season, even though there were still many questions unanswered, I praised God for beginning a change in my heart and life.

Rehearsal season began for the story ballet. I had a smaller part, and even though the rational side of me felt blessed to have it, the villain in my head couldn't wait to rub it in my face and laugh at my insignificance. **You don't even deserve this small part. You don't deserve a part in this show at all.** I tried to keep my focus from that menacing voice and dove into the themes of the show instead. It was about Tamar, Rahab, Ruth, Bathsheba, and Mary, five women in the lineage of Jesus. My mom gave me a book called *A Lineage of Grace.* It told the story of these five main characters. I read it alongside the Bible, and what really struck me about these women was how broken they were. They lived in hard situations and were far from perfect, but they made it into Christ's bloodline. I realized how similar I really was to these people, and I thought if God had a plan to use these women for greatness, maybe He could have a plan for me in my situation, too.

I continued with rehearsals and worked hard in every class. I still felt unsure of myself, but my dark thoughts were less frequent and were more often replaced with enthusiasm for the upcoming show. Every scene I had watched looked beautiful, and I loved diving in and meditating on these five passages in scripture. Even though every woman did something great, they weren't the true star of the show. Tamar and Ruth saved their families, Rahab helped protect the Israelites, Bathsheba's toxic relationship was redeemed into one that produced a wise king who built God's temple, and Mary had courage and became the mother of Jesus, but none of them were the real heroes. The only reason their unsteady lives and hard situations became significant was because of God, the true hero.

That was my turning point. One night, after thinking about this, I decided I would let God be the hero in my dance life. I still didn't know His plan for me, but I would trust He had one, and no matter what level I was in or what part I got, I would use it to praise Him humbly. I would no longer cling selfishly to my gift but place it down before His throne instead. This new outlook on everything began to change me from the inside out. I stopped wishing people would think my performance was impressive and began to pray people wouldn't notice me at all, but instead see God's love for them through my dancing. I began to enjoy myself more in classes and rehearsals, and when I felt low in my confidence, I would remind myself God had a plan for my life and this performance. I emerged into the light of God's truth after being in the darkness of my mental lies for months. Even though I had gone through an emotional rollercoaster, I'd finally found my joy.

Dress rehearsal week arrived, and I went on my school trip to a charity that fought against world hunger. Everything I had heard about it was true. I had a great time, and the things I learned there really did change my life. I was even more grateful I had the opportunity to go on this trip and dance in the ballet.

I rehearsed a bit after I returned, and then the show was there in the blink of an eye. I was a little nervous like always, but this year I felt more emboldened to share the inspiring message of the show with the audience. I walked out on the stage and experienced that amazing rush again. Reflecting on my journey to get to where I was, and thinking about how much God had changed me over the course of a year, inspired me to keep going. I danced through my weekend and was met at the end with warm hugs from my family and a sense of wonder at the true power of God.

A few weeks later, I thought everything was over when my mom rushed into my room and joyfully told me our show was going on tour to a church in Houston and asked me if I'd like to go. I felt excited, but I was also sad because the tour was during the week of my church camp. Camp had been a great spiritual experience for me in the previous year, and this time, I really did have to make a choice. The voice in the back of my head told me I didn't need to go. **They don't want you to go. You don't even have a big part.** However, one night, that voice was silenced by the Holy Spirit. I was praying over a list of prayer requests in my daily time with God, and one of the things I had prayed for was a mission opportunity. Suddenly, I realized the tour was my mission opportunity and that God had answered my prayers, and from that moment forward I knew I had to go. The negative voice in my mind was done overpowering me. It had spoken for the last time.

I finished my seventh-grade year of school, and then I was off to Houston. Our amazingly kind host homes welcomed us, and we all rested and prepared for the show the next day. I felt overjoyed because I knew from the moment I got there I had made the right decision. I was in awe of the fact God had never designed this show for one church, it was intended for two the whole time. This incredible mission trip was what He led me to through one of the hardest years of my life. I walked onstage that day with a smile. This wasn't any of my fantasies of solos or the lead role I had held onto for much too long. Instead, it was God's plan for my life, and it was perfect.

"The young women will dance for joy,
and the men—old and young—will join in
the celebration.
I will turn their mourning into joy.
I will comfort them and exchange their
sorrow for rejoicing."
Jeremiah 31:13

JACIE SELLARS

Jacie Sellars is now 15 and a student at Amarillo High School. When she's not dancing or making music, she loves to write short stories and poetry to share what God has done in her life. Since performing in Bloodline, she's had the opportunity to be in several more story ballets, and she's loved seeing the Lord at work. Her trip during rehearsal week and her tour experience helped lead her to an international mission trip to Paraguay, and she hopes to go on more mission trips in the future. She plans to keep dancing and writing for the Lord.

Full Bloom

Lou Sheldon

I held Mom's trembling hand in my own small, child's hand. Her boss looked me in the eye and asked, "Are you sure you can get her home?"

"Yes, sir," I boasted, knowing home was only a block away. He nodded, and then Mom and I left the mega-store where she worked for the small house we all lived in. Why I was there on that day at Mom's job when she had a meltdown, I don't know. And why an adult would let a child take care of someone in distress is beyond me. Maybe people had heard about my father's temper and didn't want to get in the middle of our family situation. I just knew that it was important to help my Mom feel okay, so I took her hand as she'd often taken mine.

Something happened that day between Mom and me as we walked home together. I felt responsible for her, and a lifetime of being there for her began. Sometimes by giving up time with friends or school activities to stay with her, and other times being there with her in my thoughts. While other kids talked and joked during the day at school, I wondered what Mom was doing and what she'd be like when I came home. Would she be singing Patti Page songs as she did sometimes, when Dad wasn't around, or would she be hunched into her chair watching *As the World Turns*, barely noticing me come in the door?

Lots of things happened to Mom after that critical day. Besides Mom not working anymore, her eyes changed. They didn't light up very often but usually looked lonely and scared. They reminded me of the eyes of the live baby bunny that our cat brought home in its mouth one morning. Mom's face also changed. Countless times it seemed stiff, like she was wearing a mask, hiding within herself. Once in a while, an unexpected visitor like the Avon lady would make her smile a lot, but most days she seemed so sad.

I wanted to tell someone about the bad and sad feelings in our home but didn't know who to turn to. Several of the teachers at my Catholic school went out of their way to be kind to me, but how could I put words to the emotions that engulfed me? Getting away to school each day was my one escape, and I wanted to keep it my safe place. How I dreaded entering the "Ugly Green House" (as we called our home after Dad painted it a putrid color) each afternoon. On the walk home, I would grow more and more quiet and serious, knowing that as soon as I entered our front yard, I would be "on alert" like a watchdog sniffing out danger. Numerous times I wanted to bring a friend home from school but decided against it because of the darkness of my world.

Things finally changed when I was around ten years old. Dad started talking about moving to Denver and took Mom with him to see the city. The teachers at school seemed more concerned than usual around me and sometimes their conversations ceased when I appeared. On one visit to Denver, I went with my parents. We stayed in a scary, dirty part of town with no park across the street like at home. A few months later, Dad left for Denver alone. He didn't want to live in the "Ugly Green House" with us anymore.

There was a terrible feeling in our home without Dad in it. True, his rages were unpredictable, but not having him around at all seemed worse. I missed the musky smell of his aftershave and the shininess of his shoes. They made the world I lived in a bit more bearable. The excitement of early Saturday morning fishing trips and Sunday afternoon car rides to the country no longer existed since Mom didn't drive. The melancholy echoes of country music and banging sounds from the garage as he worked in his shop were stilled.

Without Dad there, I felt even more responsible for Mom even though I didn't know how to help her during the awful months after Dad left. Mom was so pale and lifeless during that time, with dark circles under her eyes. I was afraid she might die. The little light that existed in her eyes almost disappeared. What turned the tide in Mom's favor were good people who began to step into our lives. They became the hands and feet of Jesus to someone in need. They prayed with and encouraged her, helped her to learn to drive and even provided food when we needed it. Mom's color eventually returned and her eyes began to look happier.

Some days Mom still cried over being alone and other days her expanding interest in Jesus and the Bible seemed weird. Most mornings I'd awaken to find her sitting in the living room reading her Bible and talking to "her new Husband" as she liked to call the Lord. She said she was trusting Him to take care of her. Other times, I'd hear her singing to God as she did laundry or cleaned around the house.

In all the years wondering how my mother was doing during the day, I'd never envisioned her talking to God like He was her best friend. I would've been happy if she'd just smiled more. But as a youth, I was embarrassed by her show of religious emotion. Anger, fear, or sadness I understood. Praising and joy were something new and uncomfortable. It was really appalling when Mom raised her hands in church. I just wanted to crawl under the pew. But over time, I realized it wasn't that unusual as others raised their hands to God at our new church, too.

Besides her growing interest in God, a side of my Mom that I hadn't seen since she worked at the mega-store came back. Her clothing became brighter and she invited people in for coffee and meals. Over time, I realized she was actually a very fun person to be around. Watching the transformation in my Mom was like watching an old, gnarled rose bush put out new growth under spring sunshine. Parts of it were damaged and would never grow again, but the parts of it that bloomed carried a deep, rich scent that was different from newly planted roses.

I no longer dreaded walking home from school, but instead began to bring some of my own friends home. The too tight bond between me and Mom even began to loosen as her circle of friends grew. For the few kids still at home, the atmosphere in our house was so different from what we'd known most of our lives.

Years passed and my mother continued to enlarge her world. I eventually married and started a family. Through the course of my life, I went through discouraging days of my own. Memories of how Mom had walked out of the shadowy pit her life had existed in helped me tremendously. The daily work she put into staying strong in God challenged me to do the same and keep moving forward with my life.

As my fortieth birthday approached, I contacted Mom one day, asking for information for a Grandmother's Keepsake Book for my daughter. During our visit together, she mentioned that her favorite flower as a child had been the wild pink roses that grew along the country roads she'd walked on her way to the one room school house she attended. As she reminisced, her voice was light and full of laughter even though I knew her body was wracked with pain from a disease that was quickly stealing her from us.

During the last few days she was alive, praise music filled her sickroom. One of the last things we did together was sing songs of praise to Jesus while I held her emaciated hand. Her voice was weak but full of love for her Savior who'd walked with her for so many years. Mom's body was worn out and we both knew its usefulness was over, but the assurance of a new body and the Love of her life waiting for her, helped her tremendously with the passing over process.

In her honor, pink roses cascaded over her casket. They were a salute to a woman who refused to stay hidden, but determined to bloom as best as she could, sharing the scarred beauty of who she was with those around her. And as for me, the pink rosebush in my yard keeps her bravery and love of life before me. It reminds me of her strength, fragility, and her resilience to follow God through the twists and turns of life's journey. It also reminds me to cling to the Lord each day like my mother did through prayer, praise and Bible study. As we cleaned out her home, we found scripture verses jotted on various pieces of paper stuck in drawers, on shelves, between books and other places. God's word sustained my Mom and fed her in a way that nothing else could.

Knowing that Mom is restored, the shattered parts of her whole again, comforts me when I find myself missing her. Every now and then, I swear I can hear her voice in my head praising our Savior and I know that she is having the time of her life. She is safe, in full bloom, and is waiting for me and my siblings. My job to watch out for her is over. Jesus is holding her hand now.

Molly's Progress

Deborah McCollum

Molly wrinkled her nose as she made her way past the elderly and infirm parked in wheelchairs along the nursing home corridor. She hated the harsh smell of antiseptic poorly masking the moist, rancid smell of decay that permeated the facility where Mama stayed. Hopeful faces turned towards her as she appeared, returning to blank expressions and private memories as she continued past. A few remembered her from previous visits and greeted her. Molly offered a small wave and smile with her lips pressed together. She didn't need further attachments to this place.

Molly carried a tattered reed basket, once her mother's, containing an assortment of garden vegetables. She stopped in front of her mother's door, closed as usual. She took a deep breath, prayed, "Please God, let this be a good day," and tapped her knuckles once against the white surface.

For the several seconds after she knocked, Molly tried not to hope her mother was sleeping, until a sharp, raspy voice responded. "Go away."

"Mama, it's me. It's Molly." She answered back as she pushed open the door.

Mama was seated in a recliner, looking out of a small window at the back of the room. She was dressed, which was a good sign, in a high-necked red gown, splashed with orange and yellow flowers. The gown was made with loose kimono sleeves, her preferred style. "Gives me room to move," she would tell the frustrated store clerks who only had gathered or snug-sleeved dresses on the racks. Mama often made her own clothes with the sleeves just how she wanted them. That was Mama; things always had to be just a certain way: her clothes, her home, her child, and especially her garden.

Mama turned from the view of pink flowering rose bushes and bright blue sky to give her daughter a long, hard look. "Those roses out there need to be pruned. Doesn't do any good if the dead blooms are left to fall off. We won't get any more flowers that way. You take care of that Molly, first thing."

Molly's heart soared. Mama recognized her. "Yes, Mama. I'll take care of that as soon as I go." She stood beside the recliner and laid the basket in her lap, like an offering. She watched hopefully as Mama poked at the contents.

"I brought you some vegetables. There's a bell pepper, some tomatoes and a couple of cucumbers."

"These are the saddest little things I ever saw. Where did you get such a mess?"

"Your garden, Mama." Molly scuffed her shoe against the tile like a small child. "I've been keeping the garden like you said to."

"Like I said to?" Mama shook her head. "I never said to keep a garden like this." She waved at the vegetables in her lap. "This is disgusting. These aren't fit for a pig." She knocked the basket from her lap and returned her gaze to the flowers outside. The vegetables scattered across the floor, the bell pepper rolling to a stop at Molly's feet.

Molly stood still, biting down on her lower lip to stop the sudden surge of tears and the angry urge to walk out and never come back.

"I'm sorry, Mama," she whispered. "I just don't have the knack for it, like you did- do, I mean." She darted a quick look at her mother. "And anyway, with this horrible drought and all…"

This is no drought, girl. We did better with worse many a season. Stop making excuses for yourself. It's laziness, that's all. You're not taking care of my garden like you should. And I taught you better."

"Yes, Mama. I'm sorry," One of the many of the lessons her mother had taught her was to be patient.

"Patience in the garden will teach you patience in life," Mama had said.

Molly had never been a terribly patient child, and as she grew older, her patience grew thinner. "Mama, I'm tired of this old garden. I want to play with my friends. I need to go."

She never understood Mama's attachment to that patch of ground. As soon as the March sun began to warm the earth, Mama would spend every morning in the garden. It was her daily ritual through the spring, summer and fall until late in October, when the plants finally gave up, and the earth began to harden in the cold.

"Mama?" Molly knelt beside the chair and reached out for her hands.

"What?" Those hands remained tightly clinched.

"I love you. I'll fix the garden."

Mama sighed and looked at Molly for a moment, her blue eyes clouded with confusion. "Should you be in here?"

Molly stood up. "I'm Molly Ellis, Ma'am. I was just checking to see if you're doing all right. I'll be going now." She turned to leave, wondering why it had to be like this every time.

"Wait?"

Something familiar in that tone made Molly turn back. "Yes, Mama?"

"Did you make this mess on the floor?" She gestured at the vegetables. "Because I didn't. Now I have to clean up other people's messes, too?"

Molly's shoulders slumped. "No Ma'am. I'll clean it up before I go."

"And tell someone to prune those rose bushes out there. I haven't seen one person out there taking care of them."

"I will." Molly paused at the door holding the basket of vegetables. "Bye, Mama."

The next morning, small eruptions of dust marked Molly's footsteps to the garden shed. The morning sun warmed her shoulders, and the cloudless sky promised another dry, hot day.

"Another scorcher," Molly said to the shabby gray door that used to be a bright, clean white.

In the dark interior, as Molly stood in front of Mama's tools, she said a quick, angry prayer for rain. "God, if you could spare it, a few drops would be appreciated, but more would be better appreciated." Last week, the priest had asked the church to give thanks for the spare, patchy fog they'd had early Sunday morning. "Wasn't even enough to leave the grass damp; more of a practical joke than a blessing," she remembered with fresh disgust.

Back outside, Molly trudged to the spigot to fetch the water hose and turned to study the meager garden. Exhausted tomato plants clung to rusty wire frames. Small cucumbers struggled to find shade under their own tattered leaves. The remainder of the garden looked equally dejected as it withered in the sun.

Molly knelt in front of the cucumber plants, setting the spray nozzle on the ground next to her. She dug her hands into the earth and let the dry particles of dirt trickle through her fingers as she breathed in the smell of minerals and manure. She remembered kneeling like this at Mama's side. The garden had been bountiful then, filled with life. Mama would tend her plants while murmuring prayers and encouragement. Her last task would be to lay the hose in the shadowed furrows. Water would trickle between emerald leaves, sparkling in the morning light like liquid diamonds. Mama had made gardening seem simple and beautiful.

Molly picked up the sprayer, holding it over the pathetic plants, but she didn't press the trigger. Instead, she bowed her head and wept.

This was a waste of time. She could just go to the grocery store like everyone else. She could roll her oversized shopping cart with one squeaky wheel to the produce department where green pears and orange cumquats shared space with no less than five different kinds of lettuce. She could select from a hundred perfect cucumbers in climate and moisture-controlled bins. Ruby-red tomatoes would be prepackaged in fours in square cellophaned containers. Everything would be so much easier, and Mama would never know the difference if Molly peeled off the stickers and washed away the wax. She might even be pleased with the offerings for once.

Molly opened her eyes and wiped the tears off her cheeks with dirty hands. This was not her garden, and it wasn't her mother's anymore either. A small smile played on her face as she rose from the ground, brushed the dry soil off her jeans, and turned away from the plants. "I wonder how crowded the grocery store will be this morning," she said to herself as she went to hang up the water hose.

The Choices We Make

Karin Huddleston

Once when I was five, I believed I was Wonder Woman and I flew. When reality hit—it hit hard. I needed four stitches in my forehead to recover.

Maybe that was the moment I stopped believing I could be a superhero. I stopped believing I could do anything.

When I was 12, I wanted to be a boxer, but I told myself that I couldn't because I was a girl. In high school, I wanted to play football, but I was too weak. I wanted to be a writer, but I wasn't good enough. I wanted to be a teacher, but I was too shy.

I was no Wonder Woman.

But superheroes refuse to stop fighting and refuse to compromise. Superheroes keep fighting even when they know that the fight will never end, that they can't save everyone, and that no matter how much they do it will never be enough.

I'm 40 years old now and when I look around, I realize that superheroes exist all around us. They don't wear capes. They don't have lassos of truth. They aren't bulletproof.

We see them in people like police officers, firemen, and soldiers who put their lives on the line for us everyday. Like superheroes, often with little thanks and open hostility from those they serve.

We see them in the ordinary people around us, too. In the men and women fighting addiction, homelessness, or mental illness.

We see them in those who chose healing, or teaching, or giving to others as a profession. In the mothers and fathers who fight to have children when they are told they can't. In the stepdads who step up. In foster and adoptive parents who sacrifice their own lives for those in need. In those who survive the death of a child.

Everyday these people simply make a choice to do the right thing. They make a choice to keep fighting.

I never became a professional boxer like I wanted, but I've seen Kristy Martin and Layla Ali on TV. I've had the pleasure of seeing women like Gina Carano and Ronda Rousey pave the way for other women to be successful in MMA. Strong and powerful women who made a choice to refuse to accept the status quo.

When my sons compete against a girl on the football field or wrestling mat, it makes me happy when they don't see why that's a big deal. These girls are heroes.

I've always been a writer, but in my younger days, I would tear up or burn everything that I wrote, terrified that someone would read it. In college I made a choice to show my friends silly stories that I thought no one would take seriously. When my friends did take them seriously, I made a choice to enter a poem in a contest and won second place. I entered a novel in a contest and won honorable mention.

I decided to stop working in a job I hated and became a teacher. I worked full time and raised two children while I pursued my Master's degree.

Every year, when I close up my classroom, test scores and failing students tell me that I didn't do enough. It weighs heavily on me that I didn't save them all. I have to accept that no matter how much I do—it may never be enough.

But every year I know I made a difference in at least one student's life. And isn't that how superheroes do it? One person at a time. One choice at a time.

Every year when school starts again, I know the fight is worth it. I won't don a cape and lace up boots, but I'll grab my writer's notebook and slip on my Converse. I'll remind myself that words have their own power and that bravery is just the choices that I make.

I'll pretend that I'm Wonder Woman—and I'll fly.

Karin Huddleston is an English teacher who lives in Amarillo, Texas. She has a Bachelor's of General Studies and a Master of Arts in teaching from West Texas A&M. She has been an avid reader since before she can remember and began writing short stories and poetry when she was in middle school. She has won second place and an honorable mention in the Frontiers in Writing Contest. When she is not writing lesson plans, she likes to work on her current work in progress, Memories Ghost. *She loves riding the Harley with her husband and spending time with her two sons, running them to various activities and binge watching too much TV.*

F-150

Jonathan Baker

The wind picks up and blows the old man's white hair down across his forehead. He inhales a long drag and coughs: long, sighing heaves, closed eyes. When the hacking subsides, he sets the cigarette between his lips, and it wiggles as he talks, the man rocking back, then forward again, and stopping there. He takes the cigarette and stubs it into a smoked-glass ashtray on the table beside him. His eyes turn to the west and we sit in silence. I adjust my collar, cross my legs, fold my fingers in my lap. The old man takes out a shining red pocketknife and a wedge of balsa and scratches at the wood. The crickets have begun to chirrup. The blue night descends. The old man speaks.

"I worked for everything I have, you know. Didn't have nothing handed to me. Ain't nobody around here had nothing handed to them. This land takes more than it gives. And the more you take from this land, the more it'll punish you for it."

He stabs the pocketknife into the little table, the knife jutting up from the wood, a silver gleam in the darkness. A coughing fit overtakes him—the shuddering outline of his shoulders, the piercing wheeze of his tattered lungs—and he places the cigarette to his lips again. "Suppose you might like to know why I brought you out here." The cherry crackles. "When a man knows he's going to die, he likes to talk to a preacher, ain't that so?" He scratches at his chin, the bristles rasping beneath his nails. "I know them Catholics do it, and I never did cotton to the Church of Rome, or to any church noways, but I need to talk now. Been keeping what I done inside. Time to let it out." He seems to be waiting for my approval. I uncross my legs and lean forward, place my fingers to my lips.

"Hunnerd years ago there was still Comanches on this land. They was stubborn. Took eighty years to run them injuns off this plateau. Truth is, weren't nobody ever too much interested in this empty country. Ain't nothing up here but flat. But there's good grazing lands, and oil up north, as you know." The old man lights up and sends a stream of white into the south wind. I don't know why he's brought me out here. But I will wait and listen. It's what I'm good at.

"Back in the twenties, this land gave freely. There was so much winter wheat that folks didn't rightly know what to do with it all. I tell you these things because I heard you come from the Hill Country. Ain't nobody downstate pays any mind to us flatlanders, and y'all don't know nothing 'bout the wind and the empty. But you're here now, so you ought to know.

"This land took my oldest boy from me. Sometimes I find myself angry. Ain't no use getting your dander up at a stretch of dirt, but even so, I get mad. My boy Charlie, he gave himself over to the land. Treated the soil with respect. Got up early and went to bed with the sun. A steward, as the Good Book says. Killed in a silo explosion, 1988. Took down by that same grain he spent all them years harvesting. He was a good boy. A good boy."

A long silence. "Doctor says my time's come. Ain't got more than a month, got the cancer down in my lungs. Suppose I knew it would happen this way."

The cellophane crinkles. "Never could quit these damn things." The tap of the pack, the snick of the lighter. "Never tried too hard, I guess. Seems if your time comes, ain't much a feller can do about it." In the dark, the ember glow of the Camel illuminates his face for a moment, a demon's face, with burning eyes. "I lived a good life. Had a woman. Had a son for a time."

A drag of the cigarette, a choking wheeze. "After my boy died, I weren't doin too good. My wife, she never loved me. I married her so's her father didn't kill me. I put a baby in her, you know. You play the hand you's dealt."

He leans back into his chair and I do the same, waiting. "She weren't too bad a woman in them early days. Pretty. And she could fry up a good steak, I reckon. But she never talked much, which is hard on a man. Sometime a feller wants to have a nice talk." He takes out another cigarette and lights it with the smoldering tip of the old one. "Liked to talk to my boy. He come over here sometime of a evening and we would sit out here on the porch and talk baseball and the harvest and you know. He liked to talk, and pretty good at it too. I was never no good. Like my wife."

The crickets raise their thrum. "But I sure did like to talk to that boy in the evenings."

He is coughing again, leaning forward in the rickety chair and holding his face down between his forearms. "After my boy went away, I would sit out here and let the wind speak to me. That was about the only voice I heard, the wind. It talks if you listen. But this here Panhandle wind is a angry wind. A hard wind. Says terrible things sometime."

Sitting up, he drags his Camel. "My wife, she was a quiet woman, and mean. I don't excuse what I done, but that woman, she didn't have nothing good inside her. Only good thing that ever come out of her was my boy. Sometime at night I could feel her sitting in her kitchen, I could hear the mean inside her bubblin. I know that don't sound right. But I ain't lying. I could just *feel* that ol woman sitting in there hatin me. For never workin hard enough. For turnin our boy to farmin." A cough. A wheeze. "Couldn't stand to see that ol woman glowerin at me. She could hate the skin off a rattlesnake with them beady eyes, that woman. She would just sit there and stare at me. Just starin and starin, sunup to sundown. Them black eyes. Come to be I didn't want to go in my own house. Felt I had a hex on me. My bones would ache, soon as I cast a shadow over the threshold. And them night terrors." He puffs at his cigarette. "Came time, she wouldn't come to bed no more. Just sat down in the kitchen, silent as a scarecrow." The breeze takes the smoke, sending it up into the stars.

I wait. He starts again. "The wind, it talked to me that night, told me what to do. Said a man oughtn't to be afraid to walk through his own door." The crickets have calmed. The wind whines through the porch shingles. He tugs the pocketknife up out of the table, closes it with a snap and slips it into his pocket. "My daddy give me that knife when I weren't but eight years old. I always carried it. Every day since I's eight years old. You believe that?"

"That's something," I whisper.

"It weren't nothing to open that knife and walk into that kitchen. Just like gutting a fish. She didn't scream or nothing. Silent to the very end." He takes up rocking again. I study my hands and listen to the porch boards groan beneath his rocker.

"Buried that ol woman underneath my truck," he says after a time. "Figure nobody would look under there. Reckoned they would search for her body out in the fields, if they looked for her at all. Besides, my truck is always there, I don't never go nowhere. But nobody come lookin for her noway anyhow. She weren't missed. Certainly not by me."

Out on the plain, amid the whispering grama, the crickets take up their song again. The night grows blacker and we sit in the darkness of it, right in the thickest part of it. These plains folk, they can sit forever. I have sat with killers before. But this old man is more patient than the others. Finally he says, "I s'pose I ought to drive you back into town."

I nod. We walk out to his F-150, and he starts her up, and the truck makes a heavy jolt as he backs over the bump in the dirt drive.

Three years ago, Jonathan Baker quit his publishing job in New York City and returned to his hometown of Canyon, Texas, to write full time. He currently works as a news curator for High Plains Public Radio and writes feature stories for Amarillo *magazine, and his fiction recently appeared in* (mac)ro(mic), Adelaide, *and* Hypnopomp. *He has also been featured on* The Other Stories *podcast.*

Sky with No Stars

Presley Hostetter

I suppose this is my fault. By my own selection, I stare blankly above in a room enclosed by concrete and a barred window. I suppose it is my fault for gazing wide-eyed at the glowing metro in the distance. Becoming credulous of the decorated night lights led me to be crestfallen. Bewitched by the bejeweled world of the metropolitans, I fled from a pleasant life. I fled to a sky with no stars.

An officer slides open the steel gates. His head down, chin on chest, unable to look directly at me. He stands stiff and, unlike the other officers, his posture seems forced. "Come this way," his voice beckons with timid exertion. I follow his commands and he places cuffs around my hands. We walk through a facility where lights blare a paradigmatic buzz. The facility is so well lit that the grey walls appear white. Our reflection gleams from the waxed floor and our steps echo.

With each step I huff. My chest sinks deeper and my heart pounds within me. All this pressure makes me tremble.

I came to a large city to find deep connections and enhance my world view. All it gave me was loneliness. In a placid town, the depths of night evoke serenity. The depths of night, after I rejected solitude, became discordant and hazy. In a rural town, those that dwell awake are lonely.

I argued against the ideals of Emerson, calling him a loon. I wanted to enrich my view and come to the feigned light that seemed distant. I was convinced the city was where dreams are made, ravished by the promotion of dazzling lifestyles, and assured I would find myself. My loneliness led me to indulgence. In the end, I became a caricature of Dorian Gray.

To my dismay, only disappointment came about. The decorations unraveled dissatisfaction. Nobody is pleased and equally unhappy by their own naivety that they crumble, giving into their desires. All they can do is uplift themselves to hide their sorrows. The large billboards, the facelifted women, and the lustrous lights all mask the loss of dignity. There is nothing satisfying about a sky with no stars.

Are those born inside a city locked in melancholy? Do they know what a true connection feels like? Being so condensed makes bounds ephemeral, I've come to learn. Did Icarus become so infatuated with the sun that he forgot what the stars looked like? Did he not realize the ethereal grandeur of constellations? Not even constellations choose to look over urban vanity. No magpies in the sky to carry me across the Milky Way.

The officer and I approach a leather chair equipped with belt straps. The officer stares for a second before turning to me and removing the handcuffs. "Sit there, please."

I nod. I think to myself how I've chosen to sit down, and how I equally could have chosen to attack him and flee, or how I could have stood still and made him force me into the chair, but I convince myself these actions would lead me nowhere. No matter what, I'll end up with a similar fate. I chose this fate. I didn't choose to be born, but by my actions I did choose to be faced with this penalty and a questionable penance.

The officer pulls up my sleeve, displaying my tattoo of the sun. He buckles one strap around my arm while drifting his view away from my decorated shoulder. I tense. He straps a second to my other arm, this time gentler. He has yet to look me in the eyes.

I've always pondered why others focused on creating a legacy. Once one is gone, they won't get to see any of their progress's results. Nothing should really matter to an individual, he never gets to see the world before his life or after. Being infamous or being a nobody really doesn't matter. Reaching my dreams won't be an issue once I'm dead.

"D-Do you have any final words?"

"No." I've already poisoned myself . . . what would change? There is nothing I need to say, nothing to add, and only nothing is what will resonate. I hope he doesn't feel guilty for what he's about to do. After all, this is my decision. I put myself here, and by my logic, I'm the one at fault. Nothing I can do to defend my actions. Nothing I can do to cushion my plummet. I chose to live my life, and of course any election has repercussions. Even now, I'm hurting someone.

Above me a blinding radiance glares at me. It emits a loud hum. A nudge on my decorated marking, followed by a prick. The circumference of the glare enraptures me. Mathematical truths. The blinding beam appears further away. The wings that once lifted me are dissolving. I'm drifting away from warmth and becoming encircled by darkness. I feel lifted, for I'm approaching the cosmos. Everything is weightless, as if I'm disappearing. Maybe I'll finally get to see the stars once again.

***

"How was your first outing?"

"I can't begin to think how you do this so frequently." His thumb digs deep into his index finger.

"You'll get used to it in time."

"D-d-d-o you never think about how they feel? Why was that man just now smiling?" Blood drips.

"Those thoughts will also go away in time."

"I don't want to grow cold." The blood splashes against the waxed floor.

"Maybe you'll soon learn. Clean that up before you go." He walks away, hands in his pockets, face down. The door slams behind him.

The timid officer finally looks at the prisoner resting in the chair. He blankly stares at his tattoo. "I'm sorry . . . I should've said this sooner." He closes the man's eyes, shielding him from the lamps above, and examines the smile across his face. A thought struck the officer, a revelation of sorts. *I enjoyed your last words.*

The Thing That Really Matters

Hunter Fithen

It's Bill.

Bill Mullins. But I guess you probably already know that. You also probably know what I'm about to ask, but I guess I'll ask it anyway.

What really matters in life?

I mean, really. What actually counts?

Is it our happiness? The good deeds we do? The memories we make with the people we love? Is it forgiveness, charity, or service to others?

When I was a boy, I used to love playing cops and robbers with my little brother, Henry, and watching *Magnum, P.I.* until two in the morning. I'm forty-six now and twice as hairy as Tom Selleck could ever hope to be. People always said Henry and I looked like twins, even though he was two years younger. We wanted to be sheriff's deputies.

But I never became a cop, and Henry's dead now.

Car accident. Or train accident, depending on how you want to look at it. It wasn't his fault. Wasn't the train's either.

It was mine.

Funeral was awful, seeing what I'd done to his wife and son. I kept expecting a gloomy day full of storm clouds and torrential downpour, even though the forecast said sunny with a high of 102. And windy. Henry always hated the wind.

We started our landscaping business 20 years ago, and we worked our fingers to the bone to make our dreams come true. Except they never did. For either of us. No man gets everything he wants. Few even know what they want in the first place. And you, me, and everyone else knows that if anyone deserved better, it was Henry.

Like I said, we wanted to be cops when we were kids. Bad eyes and a deaf ear kept Henry out. Bad choices and a drinking problem did it for me. He lived a semi-awful existence in school–got picked on because of his ear and glasses. I did my best to protect him. Henry never forgot that.

My brother was smart. He worked hard, shaped up to be a strong, successful man. He found a woman in college "way out of his league," as he said. She saw who he was and loved him for better or worse. That's rare in a woman. Rare in anybody. Especially nowadays. But I guess people aren't made like they used to be, right?

They got pregnant soon after marrying. Had a little boy. Baby Jake. He's fifteen now, but he'll always be Baby Jake. Henry worked twice as hard as I did. He ran the technical side of our business while raising a family.

One hell of a man, Henry was. But you already know that.

So anyway, what really matters in life? What really counts?

You know, maybe I don't need to ask you after all. Maybe the answer was in front of me the whole time.

See, the most notable thing about my brother was that he always kept his word, no matter what. I mean, we all say things we don't mean sometimes, and that's ok. It's human.

We apologize, forgive, and move on. Or at least we should. But when Henry made a promise, you know, an official commitment to something, he kept it. Not always perfectly, but he kept it all the same. You could bet on that no matter what.

And that's got to count for something.

A man is only as good as his word. That's what Henry taught me by the life he lived. A lot of things matter in life, but perhaps nothing matters more than keeping the promises we make.

The promise we make to our best friend the day we marry, to our children when they're born. The way we promise to live our lives. The promise we make to our brother the day we realize we're not invincible like *Thomas Magnum*.

I promised Henry a long time ago that if anything ever happened to him, I would look after his family.

And that promise still stands, even after I got him killed.

If I could go back, though, if I could change anything about my life, it wouldn't be Dad leaving us. It wouldn't be Mom dying of cancer. It wouldn't be not getting into the police academy. It wouldn't be the woman I loved divorcing me. No.

It'd be that my brother was still alive.

He could wake up next to his wife tomorrow, kiss her good morning. Have breakfast with his family. And he could go to work and, for once, be surprised that I'd taken care of his tasks for the day. All he'd have to do is crunch some numbers for me before going home early for the first time in his life.

He'd surprise Annie–bring flowers home for her like he did sometimes. And I'd tell him before he left the office:

"I'll pick up Jake from school today. Just text him and tell him Uncle Bill wants to go to the movies and needs someone to supervise him. You and Annie have an evening to yourselves for once, ya dork."

But I can't do that. I can't change anything about the past; no one can. And I can't face a future without him. That's why I sat by the tracks on County Road 5 yesterday with a flask in one hand and a revolver in the other.

I gambled Henry's life away.

We'd been in debt ever since mom's medical bills started showing up. We almost lost the business a couple times, but Henry found a way to get us through. This most recent paycheck was the first to put us back in the black. We were finally debt-free for the first time in years. Baby Jake had a chance to go to college.

I wanted to celebrate. I took my share of the cash profit and went to the Indian casino. My cards were hot. I'd almost doubled my money in a game of hold 'em when I went all in. The Apache man across from me called my bluff, beat my full house with a royal flush. And just like that, it was over.

Or so he thought.

I couldn't let that cash slip away. Not now. Not when I'd spent years, and I mean *years*, working my hands raw to get it. Being drunk didn't help.

I waited for the man who had beat me fair and square to come out into the parking lot. When he did, I followed until he opened the door of his *Buick*, then I put a gun to his head and told him to hand his cash over.

That's when I noticed the Apache Chieftain gang tattoo on the back of his neck.

He turned around. I wore a hunting mask, but he knew who I was. He told me to walk away before I got scalped. I pistol whipped him and took his money while he was on the ground.

Next thing I knew, I was pedal to the metal in my pickup with gunshots ringing behind me. Every shot missed. I got home, stayed up all night waiting for the cops to come for me. They never showed. Surely the man had called the police, and they had to know who I was. They'd have my physical description, and the casino had video surveillance at the poker tables. He would've described my truck, and my motive wouldn't be hard to figure out. I knew it was only a matter of time and was shocked they hadn't kicked down my door yet.

And then it dawned on me.

The Apache Chieftains didn't call the cops. They didn't want anything to do with the law. No, they handled problems on their own. I thought about that scalping comment and the rumors that the Chieftains actually did that to their enemies.

I walked around in cold sweat for the next couple weeks. Didn't leave home except to go to work. Nothing happened. I deposited the cash to my checking account, and I started to forget about it. The Chieftains didn't know my name, where I lived, anything about me. They'd probably prowled around looking for me, but if they hadn't found me yet they probably never would.

Another week passed. Life seemed back to normal. Henry called one night, said his truck broke down. I went to his house for dinner and had almost forgotten the whole thing when I remembered Henry drove an old *Chevrolet Apache.* Coincidence, I thought. But we couldn't fix it, and maybe that was a sign, huh?

That pickup was their only ride, but I had my pickup and an old Jeep at home, so I let Henry borrow my truck and he drove me back to my place.

No big deal. The next day, my brother dropped Baby Jake off at school.

That's the last thing he ever did.

When he didn't show up for work, I thought he was running late, unusual for him. Then Annie called me, bawling.

Told me to come over.

The cops said Henry got hit by a train. Annie found out through the grapevine. They weren't sure if he got stuck on the tracks, or if he parked there on purpose and waited. There was no reason for that. Things were going well for us for the first time. No reason to end it all. It was just a truck. Henry would've felt bad if it got stuck on the tracks, but he wouldn't have died for it.

The funeral was closed-casket, but I saw his body. Cops had me come to the scene to identify him. He was all torn to hell. Limbs missing, deep gashes with intestines and sinew hanging out. One thing stood out to me like nun in a liquor store. His head. I could see the white cap of my brother's skull.

All of it.

Scalped.

No way a train did that. No way that injury was so precise by chance. Cops figured likewise. Their investigation is ongoing.

The Chieftains knew my truck, and Henry and I looked very much alike. Those bastards had been on the hunt for me and found my brother instead. They must've taken him at a gas station or something on his way to work. They scalped him then set him up in my pickup on the tracks to wipe the evidence away.

I was still sitting in the dirt by those train tracks in the middle of nowhere letting the beast of my guilt chew on my soul when the blaring horn of a locomotive screamed at me and a line of boxcars chugged by my field of vision. Still clutching my *Jack Daniels* and a .357 Mag, I wondered if Henry was still conscious when the train hit, if he knew what was coming for him.

Where's the justice? I wish you, or someone out there would tell me.

As the train flew past, I watched the flickering gaps between the boxcars and tried to piece together what was on the other side. I stuck the gun in my mouth, tasting the metal as the train screamed by, the noise rattling my brain and the earth rumbling under my boots, hands shaking.

Then something snapped.

I shot up to my feet and slung my flask into the side of the train as hard as I could. I aimed my revolver at the boxcars and squeezed the trigger over and over, sending hot lead ricocheting off them until the recoil stopped and all I could hear was the faint clicking of the hammer in my ringing ears. I chunked my gun into the side of the train and fell to my knees and screamed in bitter despair.

It should have been me.

I should be the one scalped and mutilated. I should be the one in the ground right now. A victim of my own sins. Well, I am the victim of my sins after all, because now I must face the horrible reality that I've created. A fate far worse than death.

I can't live with it.

Annie. Baby Jake. They need someone to provide for them. To protect them. They need Henry.

There was only one way out of this. I had to pay the Chieftains back. If I didn't, they'd come for Annie and Jake, looking for their money. Cops couldn't find Henry's ID at the scene, which is why they called me, and I know the gang must have taken it. They knew where he lived now.

So, I got up, dusted myself off and found my revolver in the dirt. Once inside my Jeep again, I got on my phone and double-checked my life insurance policy. Henry and his family had been my beneficiary for years. I reloaded my gun and shoved it into one pocket, and a few fat handfuls of hundred-dollar bills in the other. I drove to the casino and went inside, looked around, found the Apache sitting at the same card table he'd beaten me at.

He looked amused when I sat down, like he'd been expecting me. He asked me if I wanted to play. I nodded and played the world's worst game of poker. On purpose. He got all his money back, and then some.

I told him I didn't want to play anymore. That he was too good for me, and that I was done gambling and didn't plan on ever coming back.

The Apache shrugged, and I left the table. In the parking lot, I noticed a couple of men waiting. They took me to the back alley and disarmed me, then beat me senseless. When I came to, my poker rival stood over me. He asked why he shouldn't scalp me too. I didn't have an answer. I pleaded only that he leave my brother's family alone.

He agreed there was no need to harm Annie or Baby Jake. But he couldn't let me go. He had an image to keep, and nobody rips off the Chieftains.

I accepted my fate, and now they've taken me out to the middle of nowhere, under a deep red Texas sunset. I just finished digging my own grave, and now I'm on my knees. They're letting me say a prayer before they get started.

So here I am, God.

That's my confession; that's all I have left to say. I ask you for forgiveness, but I know I don't deserve it. If I'm going to Hell here in the next few minutes, I understand. Please take care of Annie and Baby Jake. And please let Henry know that I am so sorry for what I've done.

But I have peace now. His family is safe. I promised Henry I would always take care of them if anything ever happened to him, and I've kept my word.

That's the thing that really matters, and it's got to count for something.

Amen.

Tears of a Banshee

Kim Black

Allison stared at the jewels on her left ring finger. An emerald cut into a heart shape, framed in gold, nestled between two silver hands, all topped with a crown of diamonds. Only yesterday she had turned the heart from pointing out to pointing inward during a private ceremony in the ancient Friary Chapel. The deep green stone rivaled the vibrant color that blanketed everything in Ireland.

"Friendship, love, and loyalty," she whispered as she straightened the band on her finger. She thought back to the first time she met Jeremy. Just children. He had come to her rescue when the other children taunted her. *Ginger-ginger, you have no soul!* He'd taken her hand and led her away from the others. They'd been together ever since.

"What is that you say, Mrs. Abbot?" Jeremy asked.

"Just admiring my wedding ring, Mr. Abbot."

Jeremy circled his arm around his bride's waist and drew her close for a kiss. "The jewels in your eyes out sparkle any stone on a ring." He pushed a fiery red curl back from her face and kissed her again. "And nothing is sweet to me since I've tasted your honeyed lips."

Allison blushed and gestured toward the pub at the end of the narrow stone street. "Let's get you that pint to keep you warm for our walk."

Jeremy raised his brows and shrugged. "Perhaps we could go back to the inn, and you could keep me warm enough."

"We've the rest of our lives for that, but only two more days in Ireland, and I want to see a bit before we go." She led him up the steps of the century-old tavern and through the blackened oak door.

The dark pub smelled of ale and smoke. Allison struggled to understand the locals as they chattered and laughed over frothy pints. The couple took a table near the door and waited for service. Allison couldn't help but smile. Jeremy looked like a jack-o-lantern, his broad grin glowing from one ear to the other. Pure joy.

A young man in a slouched beanie approached. "Can I bring you a pint?"

"Just one—Guinness," Jeremy said with a nod. "And a cup of tea for my wife."

The young man turned and raised his chin toward the bar. "Pint o' Black and a Scald," he yelled above the din. He twisted to face Jeremy again. "Give me a minute." He didn't wait for a response before jumping to the next table.

True to his word, Beanie was back in only a minute with Jeremy's beer and Allison's tea.

"Thank you," Allison said.

"Grand."

Jeremy coughed his way through the stout ale at the same pace as Allison sipped her too-hot tea. "So where is this scenic trail we're supposed to take? I didn't see any signs outside." He scanned the room. "Do you think anyone here knows it?"

Allison shrugged and gestured to Beanie as he rushed past their table. "Excuse me, can you help us?"

"What's the story?"

Allison looked at the young man and drew an excited breath. "We were told there was a walking trail near here. One with a waterfall. Can you tell us how to find it?"

Beanie's expression turned somber. He looked back to the barman and shrugged.

The old barman shook his head a fraction of an inch. "If the Yank goms want to go, let them." He tossed a white towel over his shoulder and looked away.

Beanie leaned over their table and whispered. "The waterfall trail is up the road half a kilo and to your right. But it's not much to see this time of year. I'd advise don't waste the day. Stay here, and I'll bring you afters. We have a nice pie in the back my maw made this morning."

Jeremy shook his head. "No, thank you. We're on our honeymoon. For my part, I got to visit a real pub and enjoy a pint of Guinness. For Allison, we're taking a walk on this waterfall trail. Is it half a kilometer to the right or left from the door."

Beanie looked at Allison and frowned. "It's not a nice place, Miss."

Jeremy pulled out money enough for the bill, and then a few Euros more. He pressed them into Beanie's palm. "Right or left?"

The man tossed the bribe back on the table. "Left." He nodded to them both and hurried away.

Jeremy shrugged and rose to his feet. He pulled out Allison's chair and took her hand as they left the tavern. "Strange, wasn't it? And I didn't like the looks he was giving you."

Allison took a deep breath of the cool April air. "You're jealous, love." She turned left, toward the west, as soon as they reached the road. "We've just enough sunlight left."

Jeremy pushed his elbow out, and Allison looped her hand around it as they walked. In just a few minutes, they reached a clearing in the overgrowth to the right of the street. A sign labeled "Morrigan Falls Trail," as well as something else in Gaelic, directed them down an ancient path in the green wood.

Jeremy helped Allison over several fallen logs and under the moss-covered gnarls of ancient tree branches. The stones underfoot became damp. After another ten minutes, they could hear the roar of falling water. And something else.

Coming around a blind corner, Allison could see the falls. White and gurgling and screaming with energy. It was more than just the water screaming.

"What is that?" Allison asked. "That dreadful screeching? Where is it coming from?"

Jeremy swiveled his head and shrugged.

Allison looked all around them. The pool at the base of the falls was at least fifty yards across at the narrowest point. The water was black as pitch once the ripples calmed. Across the pool from them was the falls. It was a wall of black granite divided by a white gash of liquid fire. The rush was so intense that Allison felt the force from the other side. Her stomach felt heavy. The screaming continued.

She scanned up the falls to the crest, where she saw a woman to one side, on her knees.

Allison grabbed hold of her husband's arm and squeezed. "Jeremy, do you see her?"

Jeremy looked up, shielding his eyes from the last direct rays of the sun. "I see something. I'm not sure it's a person."

"It's a woman. She's upset. Can't you see? We have to help her. There must be a way up." Allison looked around for another path. She saw nothing along the trail from where they came. She hurried around the bend in the pool. "I think I found a way."

Jeremy ran up after her. "Please don't run off without me. There could be snakes or something."

Allison shot him a flustered look. "This is Ireland. No snakes, remember?"

Jeremy smiled and stuck out his tongue. "I don't know what you think we're going to accomplish by going up there."

"We can get her down. It's dangerous up there. She's obviously upset about something. Maybe we can help." Allison was losing her breath as they climbed up the less-defined trail on the other side of the falls. As she looked back down to the pool, she saw clearly that the rushing column of water came down on a tremendous pile of jagged boulders, sheared from the cliff's face centuries ago. Worry overtook her whole body. "We can't let her fall."

Jeremy scanned the trail ahead and took Allison's hand. "Maybe we can help."

As they came near the top, the trail disappeared into the rocks. Jeremy climbed ahead of Allison, pulling her up to the next tier.

Where the rocks ended, a thick green forest began. Allison searched for the woman.

They both saw her at the same time. From below, she was a gray silhouette, but from where they stood, just a few paces from her, she looked like a fairy. The woman knelt on a broad flat rock at the side of the river. Her long white dress was soaked and clung to her body. Blonde hair nearly as white as her dress hung like a curtain over her face, and she keened back and forth, sobbing hysterically.

"Can we help you?" Allison asked.

The woman in white stopped her crying immediately and looked up at the couple with round black eyes, rimmed with scarlet from her tears. "None can help me."

Jeremy looked at the young woman as though he was embarrassed to interrupt her mourning. He glanced toward Allison and then back at the woman. "We heard you crying. We didn't mean to scare you, but we'd like to help."

The woman seemed to respond to Jeremy's voice. Her eyes softened. She stood and took slow, fluid steps in his direction. The translucent dress accentuated every curve of her body. She shivered.

Jeremy quickly removed his jacket and draped it over her shoulders. "You're like ice."

Allison pressed closer to his side. "What's wrong? Can we help you? I'm Allison, and this is my husband, Jeremy." She emphasized *husband*. Jeremy was always eager to help anyone in need.

The woman continued to shiver, her gaze locked with Jeremy's. "It's been a year, and I canna' get over my loss." Her Irish accent danced with her sorrowful tone. "I lost my bonny. He was tall and strong like you. With a soft heart. I dunna' think I can live without him." She shifted her eyes away to stare over the edge of the falls.

Allison shook her head, holding fast to Jeremy's arm. "Please don't hurt yourself. You're young and beautiful. You have your whole life ahead of you."

The woman looked back to Jeremy. "Do you think I'm beautiful?"

Jeremy fixed a dubious expression on his face. He glanced at Allison and then back to the woman. "Of course, you're beautiful."

"And you think I have hope to love again?" The woman pulled Jeremy's jacket tightly around her.

Jeremy nodded. "I should think so."

Allison stepped forward, reaching toward her. "Please, come back to town with us. We can get you help."

As soon as Allison stepped forward, the woman stepped back like a frightened cat. She shook her head again. "I am alone. You will take me back and then leave me with strangers. I will be alone again."

Jeremy reached out toward her. "No, you come back with us. We'll do whatever we can to help. Come on, now. Please."

Allison felt a knot growing in her stomach. She didn't know if it was jealousy or something else. She wished she had listened to the boy at the pub. She wished they hadn't come.

The woman stared at Jeremy's outstretched hand. She took a tiny step in his direction. She held up her hand, just beyond his reach. Allison saw that she wore a Claddagh ring on her finger, too. It wasn't as lavish as Allison's, but the silver band gleamed in the dying sunlight.

Allison felt ashamed of her suspicion. Jeremy wanted to help this woman—at her request. The woman had lost the love of her life. Allison couldn't imagine living without Jeremy. He protected her. He was there for her. He was her life. Her love. Her everything.

"Allison, stay back. The rocks are slick here." Jeremy pulled his arm from Allison's grip to take another step toward the woman.

"Be careful, love," Allison whispered.

Just as Allison's hand slipped from Jeremy's arm, the woman in white flashed a wicked smile and lunged toward Jeremy. Allison screamed helplessly as she watched her new husband and the woman fly over the edge of the cliff and disappear into the raging foam below.

Allison searched through the thick mist but could see nothing. She could hear nothing but the screeching of the woman in white.

But the woman in white was gone. Jeremy was gone. The screaming was all that remained.

She couldn't move. She couldn't think. She had to get help, but she couldn't leave. And who would come? Who could help her now?

Allison dropped to her knees, keening and wailing on the rocks at the head of the falls. She felt the color drain from her face. Her hair. Her soul. Amid the screaming, in the back of her mind, she thought she heard a whisper.

"Friendship, love, and loyalty."

Kim Black is an award-winning, multi-genre author. Under both Kim and Kimberly Black, she has self-published multiple historical Christian novels, cozy suspense novels, and children's books. She also has a character creation workbook for writers. Drawing inspiration from the women in her family and in her circle of friends, Kim's work focuses on smart, strong female characters facing life-changing situations. Kim lives in the Texas Panhandle with her husband, children, and extended family.

She blogs, Living Write, on her website, www.kimblackink.com, where she also shares some of her short stories.

Facebook: facebook.com/KimBlackInkAuthor/

Twitter, Instagram, and Pinterest: @KimBlackInk

Amazon: amazon.com/Kim-Black/e/B079BYN359/

Biography of the Wolf Lady

Coby C. Spurrier

Few historic figures are viewed as unambiguously evil, but Katina, the so-called Wolf Lady of Dragonsrest, surely qualifies for that dishonor. Born to the Tront Family in the two hundred sixty-seventh year of the second age, Katina was presented to her grandfather, High King Mearden Tront II, a famously kindhearted man who viewed the solemn, intense babe and whispered, "She looks like a she-wolf ready to pounce."

Katina's childhood in the capital city of Ablion was difficult from the start. Her father, Prince Albert Tront II, and her mother, Aika, showed little affection for their brood. Her eldest step-brother, Austu, sixteen at Katina's birth, was a drunkard and womanizer, infamous in the Kingdom. Her younger brothers, Cephorus and Magnus, were born much later, so for years she was the only child in the Royal Court.

By the age of 14, Katina was a famous beauty with many suitors. She was married to cement relations with Lord Regent Haku of the City-State of Dragonsrest. She entered the court, it was said, as a pawn, but quickly became a queen. The elderly Lord Haku loved her and allowed her all the power she wished.

When Mearden Tront II died the following year, her father was made High King, and he faced a greatly depleted treasury, thanks to his father's poor management. Albert II dismissed the High Council, forcing them to buy back their positions. In the year 297, after many miscarriages, the Lady of Dragonsrest gave birth to a son, who she named Mearden after her grandfather. Haku quickly made Mearden his heir, but the Lady had much larger ambitions for her child.

Two years later, Albert II died—many say poisoned by a vengeful former Council member—and his son, Katina's brother Austu, took the throne. At age forty-eight, Austu's wild seeds had yet to be sown, and the history books are nearly pornographic in their depictions of life at the Royal court during the years of his reign. Katina, whose passion was for power not fornication, was scandalized every time she visited Ablion.

Haku, Lord of Dragonsrest, died the springtide after Albert II. Mearden III ascended to the throne, ruling jointly with his mother. Doubtless, Mearden had the right and would have preferred to rule alone, but Katina convinced him that his position was only temporary. He would have the Dragton Kingdom, not merely a nomadic city. In Castle Dragonsrest, she entertained dozens of diplomats from areas around the Forbidding Desert, sowing seeds of discontent. Her guest list over the years expanded to include the Emperor of Arcadia and the rulers of Iiauskana as well.

For thirteen years, Austu ruled Dragton, and proved an able leader despite his moral laxity. Several historians point to proof that Katina cast the spell that ended her brother's life, but evidence one way or another is lost in the sands of time. In any event, both she and her son Mearden were visiting the royal court in the year 312 when Austu died, and immediately challenged the rule of his daughter and heir, Amanda.

Katina's speech to the High Council is perhaps helpful to students of public speaking. She began with flattery and self-abasement: "My most august and wise friends, members of the High Council, I am but a provincial lady, and I can only assume to bring to issue what you yourselves must have already pondered."

She continued on to praise the late High King, a popular ruler in spite of his flaws: "He was a true Tront and a great warrior, destroying—with your counsel—the near invincible army of Arcadia."

She wasted little time before coming to her point: "High Queen Gysilla unfortunately did nothing to temper my brother's lustful spirits. Had she attended to her duties in the Imperial bedchamber more faithfully, we would have a true heir to the Kingdom, not the halfwit, milksop bastards who call themselves the High King's children. The girl Amanda is popularly believed to be the daughter of Gysilla and the Captain of the Guard. It may be that she is the daughter of Gysilla and the boy who cleans the cistern. We may never know for certain. We do know the lineage of my son, Mearden. The last of the Tront Dynasty."

Despite Katina's eloquence, the High Council allowed Amanda to assume the throne as the High Queen Amanda II. Katina and Mearden returned to the Forbidding Desert and began assembling the rebellion.

Details of the War of the Dragon Throne are included in other histories: we need not recount the High Queen Amanda's capture and eventual execution in the marshlands in the year 314, nor the ascension of Katina's son, Mearden III, seven years later. Her surviving brothers, Cephorus and Magnus, fought the High King and his mother for years, tearing the Kingdom apart in a civil war.

When Mearden III fought his uncle Cephorus in Arcadia at the Battle of Laurina Plains in 327, Katina was fighting her other brother, Mearden's uncle Magnus, in the Forbidding Desert at the Battle of Scorpion Keep. She received word of her son's defeat and capture just as she was preparing to mount an attack on Magnus's weakest flank. The sixty-one-year-old Wolf Lady flew into a rage and led the assault herself. Magnus and his army fled under the onslaught. In the midst of the victory celebration, Katina learned that her son the High King had been killed by an angry mob before his trial in Riverton, burned to death within his carriage.

When Cephorus was proclaimed High King, Katina's fury was terrible to behold. She summoned demons to fight for her, had her necromancers resurrect her fallen enemies as undead warriors, and mounted attack after attack on the forces of High King Cephorus I. Her allies deserted her as her madness grew, leaving only her companions of zombies and skeletons she had amassed over the years. The City-State of Dragonsrest became a land of death. Stories of the ancient Wolf Lady being waited on by rotting skeletal chambermaids and holding war plans with vampiric generals terrified her subjects.

Katina died at the age of 70 after a month long siege on her castle in the year 337. While she lived, she had been the Wolf Lady of Dragonsrest, Daughter of High King Albert II, Wife of Lord Regent Haku, Aunt of High Queen Amanda II, Mother of High King Mearden III, and Sister of High Kings Austu and Cephorus. Three years after her death, Cephorus died, and his and Katina's brother Magnus took the throne.

Her death has hardly diminished her notoriety. Though there is little direct evidence of this, some theologians maintain that her spirit was so strong, she became a demon after her death, inspiring mortals to mad ambition and treason. It is also said her madness infused Castle Dragonsrest, and that it infected the next lord to rule there. Ironically, that was her 18-year-old nephew Albert, the son of Magnus. Whatever the truth, when Albert left Dragonsrest in 345 to assume the title of High King Albert III, he quickly became known as Albert the Mad. It is widely rumored that he murdered his father Magnus.

The Wolf Lady must surely have had the last laugh.

No Books!

Janda Raker

"Want to go kayaking in Newfoundland?" Lyle asked one day in 2003. Not even knowing where Newfoundland was and not wanting to admit that to my adventurous husband, I said, "Sure. When?" That was before the internet, so I hurried to the encyclopedia to clear up the mystery. It would be a long trip from Amarillo! And so we began to plan. We included many other cool adventures along the way, but Newfoundland was the ultimate destination—or at least the farthest from home on that trip.

The father of a friend had a small guide service on the east coast of Newfoundland—a large, beautiful island part of the easternmost Canadian province, north from Maine past the Maritimes. He would have been happy to guide our tour, but we—being very experienced kayakers and campers and being frugal—really didn't need a guide, just direction. We had our own tandem sea kayak, a 17-foot Folbot, a foldable skin-on-frame craft that we'd paddled in many waters across the U.S., so no equipment was needed. It would be romantic to find a small island within paddling distance of the mainland, somewhere isolated enough to avoid encounters with other people. My friend contacted her dad, who was willing to recommend a destination in that northern Atlantic area.

Lyle and I loaded our necessities into our Jeep Cherokee, with kayak on top, mountain bikes on the back, and backpacker tent and sleeping bags inside. As usual, I included a travel/adventure book and a couple of outdoor magazines to read and some material to write on, as I was an aspiring travel writer. And we had developed a habit of reading a book of common interest aloud to each other in the car as we drove, so we packed a couple of novels. For several weeks that summer, we drove east across the U.S on I-40—from Amarillo near the middle to Knoxville, Tennessee, from the flat, windy High Plains across rolling hills with rivers and lakes, and through valleys surrounded by deep forests.

In the evenings in campgrounds across the country, I wrote by flashlight outlines and details about the terrain we were crossing, for travel articles. From the end of I-40, we motored through Appalachia, past New York City and Boston, through Bar Harbor in Maine, and then into Canada, covering New Brunswick, Prince Edward Island, and Nova Scotia, including beautiful Cape Breton Island and the quaint little community of North Sydney. There, with our Jeep on the large, convenient ferry, we had a beautiful, cool, rainy, six-hour voyage across Cabot Strait to the vivid green shores of Channel-Port aux Basques, Newfoundland, on the southwestern tip of the island. Whenever we're on a boat, of any size, both of us make it a habit to spend as much time as possible out on deck, peering at the water, looking for marine critters, experiencing the weather, smelling the salty air, watching for other water craft, and just catching the view. This trip was beautiful.

Having covered more than 3,500 miles to reach Newfoundland (Newfound*land* rhymes with under*stand*), we then spent several more days motoring and camping nearly 600 additional miles across that rugged, scenic island. It's shaped something like the letter "h," and we docked on the bottom left and wanted to reach the bottom right, out on the Avalon Peninsula, almost an island itself. Along the south, craggy cliffs, numerous little bays, and rivers running across the highlands and down into Cabot Strait and the North Atlantic create a coastal area of about 200 miles through which no roads cross. Many small villages are accessible only by boat. So it was necessary to drive the hump of the "h" to reach the southeastern corner. The highway headed north through Corner Brook, east to Springdale and Gander, and then turned southeast onto a narrow isthmus leading out along the easternmost coast of Newfoundland. We stayed south of St. John's, going down the southeastern shore, details of which I documented each evening. By then, we were about 400 miles east of Maine in the North Atlantic.

The native caribou I kept watching for along the highway never came into view. However, the rugged windswept ridges and small pockets of forest—red pine, paper birch, and mountain ash—interspersed with barren hillsides and tiny lakes, were entrancing. Finally, early one afternoon, we reached the town of Cape Broyle and stopped at the little guide shop near there—a tiny, rugged wooden structure, one-bedroom-house sized with many-paned windows. Talking with the owner, the father of our friend, we let him know what we had in mind. At our ages at that time—I had just passed sixty, Lyle in his mid-sixties—we could paddle our kayak only a few miles a day, but we had in mind to go to a small, uninhabited island to camp for a few nights, and then come back to where we'd launched. The rugged but efficient man provided laminated maps for members of groups he guided or for folks he outfitted, but for $5 he would loan us one with directions to the recommended tiny haven for our trip.

He was enthusiastic and wished he were going. From his description, the island sounded perfect. It apparently didn't have a name, but only a few miles drive from his office was needed to arrive at a parking area near a launch site for our craft, which would hold all our gear for several days. We could paddle—a couple of hours or less in good weather—to a cove on the islet.

As he described it, the isle was not much larger than a traditional city lot back home in Amarillo. The northern shore, our destination, was gravel with an arc-shaped beach about thirty feet deep in the center and maybe seventy feet across. The backdrop to the beach was a gray, rock cliff about forty feet high in the center, tapering down to ten feet or so at each end. That cliff prevented our going to visit the rest of the island, unless we used our kayak and went around. But it also made the island seem more interesting, adding an element of mystery as to what might lie on the other side of the cliff. And if it rained, our host explained, the western end of the cliff was the drainage for a small stream that would form a nice little waterfall—

and cool shower—twelve or more feet high. The guide even gave us a free tide table for the area, so we'd know what to expect and when. The average tides would be one meter—not much more than three feet—and with a slanted beach, pulling our boat above the tide line would be easy.

Happy with his description, we paid him the $5 and agreed to bring the map back to his business a few days later. If his office was closed, we were just to slide the map under the door. So pleasant and easy to deal with, like most Canadians.

On the way to our Jeep Cherokee, the two of us discussed how long to stay out. Three nights seemed ideal to us both. And I privately decided to forego my usual baggage of writing materials and books to concentrate on the experience, on spending time with Lyle, on just enjoying the adventure. We quickly packed our necessities for the next three days in our craft, donned our life vests, and launched from the sandy shore.

As advertised, the paddling was easy, with a slight breeze in our faces and the temperature in the low seventies. Between paddle strokes over the gentle, one-foot swells, we watched for orcas, dolphins, even seals, but nothing broke the surface of the water except a few mid-sized fish leaping for insects. Various gulls cruised overhead, apparently checking us out, and occasionally calling out to their companions.

Several small, rocky islets were visible in the area, but by following my compass we could soon tell which island to head for. The effort of paddling felt good and the invigorating scent of salt water pervaded. The island neared sooner than we'd have wished. Paddling around to the northern side, then closer to shore, we slid the bow up onto the large gravel and broken shells. Being seated in front, I hopped out, grabbed the bow line, and pulled the boat farther onto the shore. A perfect little resort for the next few days, with the light gray, slick rock cliff as backdrop.

We unloaded our gear, chose the eastern edge of the beach for our base, and erected our little gray-and-gold backpacker tent near a few chair-sized rocks. Halfway between the shore and the cliff wall, we were well above the tide line, which was obvious from the row of seaweed, small shells, and other debris. The north side of the island would be analogous to our front yard, with the sea being the street, the cliff being our house, and the side of the island beyond the cliff representing our backyard. The layout felt familiar. Opening our dry bags, I accessed ingredients for our "cracker dinner"—the light meal of the day consisting of crackers and canned meat, peanut butter, dried apricots, and other such morsels. Though our journey hadn't been far, we'd worked up quite an appetite. After eating our quick lunch and rinsing our utensils in the surf, Lyle went into the tent to spread out our Therm-a-Rest mattresses and double, zip-together sleeping bag. I knew well what would happen next—he'd soon be taking his afternoon nap in the cool, ventilated shade of the little tent.

Which was fine. With our little cove to explore, I took the opportunity to look for flotsam and jetsam on the beach, and to inspect the base of the cliff to see what the intermittent waterfall had created. All that took about twenty minutes, including picking up trash from the tide line. It was before the plethora of plastics, so there were only a couple of beer-bottle tops, a pop-top tab, and an old Vienna-sausage can, which were soon placed in a plastic grocery-store bag that would be our trash bag for the trip. Then what?

Sitting back on a pale patch of sand halfway up the beach, I watched the deep blue waves for marine life. Nothing appeared. The tide was coming in, as the tide table foretold, the water about four feet inland from its low point for the day. I scanned for boats but didn't see any, then glanced at my water-resistant watch wondering if Lyle would soon be up from his nap. Not yet. I walked along the small stretch of shore again, to check for more debris. Nothing except a few bits of seaweed and broken shells. A low rock near the tent beckoned, so I sat and watched puffy clouds sliding north over the shore on the mainland, still visible in the distance. The sky around them was brilliant blue.

Suddenly I began to panic. All these details, but I feared forgetting them. How necessary paper and pen were to take notes, to jot down details, to recall the environment, the experience. And books! During quiet time, I needed to be reading about sea-and-island adventures, to have examples of vocabulary pertaining to this activity, to access active verbs and descriptive adjectives. I couldn't stand it. I felt stranded, isolated, disconnected. Before all were equipped with cell phones and iPads, I'd failed to consider what to do with my thoughts, how to preserve them. And what to do during Lyle's nap time.

I refrained from waking him to explain my discovery, but as soon as he roused ready for our supper of freeze-dried Pad Thai using water we'd brought in plastic jugs and would heat on our tiny backpacker stove, I told him my revelation, that it would be impossible for me to stay out there on our lovely island for three nights because I had *no books* and no paper and pen! We'd have to return to our vehicle the next day.

Of course, Lyle was amazed, had had no inkling of my distress. He was happy as a clam—if clams are happy and enjoy taking naps. He'd thought of my writing as an optional activity—I could do it or do without it. And perhaps I had too. But I'd just realized that was not true. Writers *need* to write. Once an idea hits, it's painful to allow anything to prevent the writing from happening.

What had the ancients done, those before writing? They'd been the storytellers, building the big fires at night and regaling the audiences—the followers in their communities—with their versions of the story, adventures in words and actions, adjectives and verbs. But those storytellers had audiences who wanted to hear from the wordsmith. And by telling the story to a group, there was the likelihood that someone else would pass on the story, perhaps with some faint modification, but who would never let the story die. And others would come, storytellers from other places with other experiences and adventures. Stories would be traded, elaborated on.

But I had an audience of only one—a person who took afternoon naps and, following a good paddle, would be ready for bed shortly after sunset. And so my stories would die without paper to save them on. And without storytellers from other locales coming to tell their stories—the books usually brought along—my stories would not be enriched, I would not be able to learn from the tales of others.

I was disappointed, sorry not to be able to fulfill my "contract" and stay the time we'd agreed on. As happened occasionally, I'd come to the point of telling myself, "Be careful what you want, 'cause you might get it." I'd wanted three nights on a little "desert"—meaning "deserted"—island without books, without paper and pen to write on. But I rapidly found myself discontent with such a constraint.

Lyle knew he could take a nap anywhere and would be able to explore our side of the island in that one evening. He wasn't upset to relinquish the other two nights on the lovely shore. He never really related to my need to share my stories, but he humored me. And the next day, the two of us happily paddled back across the tranquil stretch of sea to our vehicle and my bag of paper and pen . . . and books!

Blondielocks and the Three Bears

KJ Waters

My first ever adventure at Yellowstone National Park began dramatically. Within ten minutes of entering at West Yellowstone, my husband spotted a grizzly bear about seventy-five yards away across a shallow part of the Madison River, a big one at 500 pounds or so. My kids (12, 10 and 4 years old) and I grabbed our cameras and jumped out of the car and stood along the opposite bank in awe watching the bear meander down the steep slope. Our excitement grew as he approached a tree and lazily scratched his back along the rough bark.

I kept a close eye on the animal knowing that a grizzly bear can run as fast as a racehorse. It would only take him a few seconds to reach us if he wanted to—luckily, he ignored us. We filmed him calmly walking along the bank of the river before he disappeared up the hill into the thick forest.

As we climbed back in the car, I noticed the kids' comatose look from days on the road had disappeared, replaced by a look of enchantment. The Yellowstone they'd heard about for months was finally a real place, not just a picture in a book. We were astonished at our luck and tried to explain that people spend weeks in Yellowstone and never see a grizzly bear. Seeing a bear in the wild was an immense thrill; the glory of the beast but also the danger that he could attack at any moment.

We had our next sighting five minutes later at a pullout where several cars were parked. The people gathered around were looking up intently. We found a bright white mountain goat way up on the cliff effortlessly clinging to the rocks. A few quick pictures and we excitedly continued on our way through Yellowstone to the north entrance at Mammoth Hot Springs. Our eyes were eager for more animals with all of us searching the forests and meadows as we drove.

Enormous bison, nearly as big as our van, munched grass along the roadside. One raised his tail and stepped toward my open window, snorting as I took a picture. The dude was pissed. We watched him cross behind the canoe we were pulling and charge a male bison on the other side of the road. I lost track of him as we drove around a curve, my heart beating fast.

A puff of what we thought smoke greeted us around a bend—it was steam rising from the ground at Mammoth Hot Springs and the smell of sulfur and rotten eggs permeated the car.

Rounding the corner brought an amazing sight—a pure white hillside with tinges of yellow, and steam rising all around. The mineral deposits from millions of years built up to create, in places, what looked like the surface of the moon. Now we were all enchanted.

Near the shops and hotels around Mammoth, a female elk waited at the crosswalk looking as if it were one of the tourists. My imagination added a hat and shawl. I then took in more elk and their newly born calves lounging on the grassy knolls between buildings as if waiting for the picnic to arrive.

We'd entered a magical land with surprises around every corner. The surreal landscape changed from thick hilly forest when we had first entered the park, to meadows and rolling hills, to the strange vistas of dirt-covered hills with rocky crags poking out here and there near Mammoth. How could there be so many different landscapes in one place?

We got out of the car and on our way to lunch found a park ranger. Bubbling with excitement, we told him of our grizzly sighting. Impressed, he told us he hadn't seen a grizzly yet this season despite being in the park nearly every day. One of his duties was to hold bear talks with visitors. He knew all the places a person might spot one and told us 150 grizzly bears live in Yellowstone's 2.2 million acres. To see one was rather like finding a needle in a haystack.

We exited the park after lunch and headed north to a cabin along the Yellowstone River where we set up for the week—a gorgeous spot with mountain vistas all around. We saw a mass of cars pulled over while driving between Canyon and Mammoth. We parked along the road and walked a hundred yards or so to see what the hubbub was.

A grizzly slept in the grass in the shade of some pines about seventy-five yards away, relaxed and oblivious to the thirty or so gawking humans. After about ten minutes it startled awake, probably due to some kids running back and forth noisily across the road. Their parents could have used the talk from our ranger friend about being quiet and walking in tight groups near a bear. Running triggers their attack response much like a dog wanting to chase a rabbit.

The bear stood and looked right into my eyes, or so it seemed. This time the protection of our car was out of reach. With cute, delicious short blonde people wanting to run away, we decided, in a tight group, to slowly beat feet back to the car, not wanting to be one of the few bear attacks each year. We were beyond relieved to return to the safety of the car.

The next day the sunrise greeted us with a spectacular display over the mountains. The day would prove to be incredible—outdoing our first day by a mile. We drove south from our cabin along the Yellowstone River in Montana to enter Wyoming again as we made our way toward Old Faithful.

Cars jammed a parking lot near the petrified tree parking lot, so we decided to see what the commotion was about. We noticed a national park film crew van as we exited the car and made our way down a wooded path, excited for what we might find. Down the road a crowd of people gathered around a ranger's pickup truck. A magical moment was afoot—a mother black bear and her two cubs were lying under a tree about twenty-five feet down a hill.

The ranger welcomed us by saying, "You are witnessing a once in a lifetime scene." He had tears in his eyes that made him even more convincing. "I've been watching this mother bear in the area for years. This is the first time I've seen her with twins," he whispered excitedly. "She is usually hiding the cubs because of the grizzlies. She was standing up not fifteen minutes ago nursing the cubs when I got the call."

We watched the trio lying in the grass, cubs asleep with the mother keeping a drowsy watch in case anyone in the crowd had bear-napping on their minds. A nice man in the front of the crowd moved aside and let my kids get closer so they could get a better look. Lady Luck was with us again. I promised to pay her in chocolate if she kept hanging around.

"Sir, ma'am." The ranger stopped a couple who were attempting to walk down the road toward the petrified tree. "You need to walk slowly in tight groups. We don't want the mother bear agitated." The couple waited patiently for more people to join them down the path.

I was curious and asked him about it. He answered, "Bears don't have very good vision. If they see a large group they won't view it as prey. They ignore it as something too big to eat."

That clarified the danger Yellowstone held knowing that the bear could happily eat any of us if she so desired. I held my four-year-old daughter's hand a bit tighter and pulled her closer. "I thought we weren't allowed to be within a hundred feet of a bear in the park?" I asked. The warnings were posted everywhere, and each summer hikers and campers were attacked as proof of the need for the signs.

"You're not. That's why I'm here to control the situation." He touched the bear spray and pistol on his belt. "I've asked everyone to keep calm and follow proper bear etiquette." An image of Goldilocks came to mind with her poor treatment of the bears.

"She must have mated with a cinnamon bear to have two cubs of such a different color. In the fifteen years I've worked in this park I've never seen it." He was very chatty, and I picked his brain for fifteen minutes until the mother bear began eyeing the crowd. We decided to not be greedy and moseyed off to see Old Faithful.

I wanted to make sure Lady Luck stuck with us, so I had her pick whatever she wanted of the chocolates from the gift shop. I got a delicious coffee to sip on as we watched Old Faithful spew its magic minutes after we stepped outside. On our return visit, just down the road from the petrified tree, several cars were again pulled over. We made a parking spot—against park rules since we were partly blocking the road—and walked toward the crowd.

A cinnamon bear cub clung to the top branch of a tree, swaying back and forth forty feet in the air. With the help of a spotting scope, we saw the mother black bear resting under the tree. It had to be the three bears we'd seen earlier. The coloring was the same, black mama and cinnamon baby. The second cub was not in sight and we hoped a grizzly hadn't gotten to him. Likely something had scared the cub up the tree a while ago, given the relaxed state of the mama bear.

A ranger interrupted our discussion and politely asked us to move our car. We obliged and made our way to the lodge for lunch where we clicked through our cameras to see if we got any good shots. None of us did. That night we drove through Lamar Valley on the northeastern side of Yellowstone. A herd of pronghorn skipped through the tall grass along the river and bison roamed contentedly. Where were the deer? That was all we needed to capture the essence of the old song.

A few snapshots and we continued our way along the beautiful landscape. We stopped at a picnic area where a few people were talking eagerly down by the stream.

"What's going on?" I asked, following their gaze into the woods.

"We just saw a bear beyond that crooked tree." The man pointed up the hill across the shallow stream.

"Heading away from us, right?" I asked while looking down at Shorty and holding her a bit closer.

"Who knows? He could double back," the man said. "It's our first bear sighting. We got here a month ago and haven't seen one yet! Did you see the claw marks on the tree near the outhouse?"

I hadn't but would check it out on our way back to the car. I told him of our grizzly sighting the first five minutes in the park and the mama and cinnamon bears from earlier in the week. They looked at us in astonishment. Shorty backed me up, shyly nodding and saying, "The baby bears were so cute."

We talked for another few minutes and decided to find the rest of our family. As we walked away, I asked Lady Luck to consider a donation to this couple. We had been blessed with an abundance so far. Not that I was complaining. She smiled and pointed upstream. The rest of our group was there with a gaggle of die-hard naturalists. Two of them had spotting scopes and generously let us gawk into them.

My mother-in-law hogged one scope, talking a mile a minute. She fit right in with the die-hards, being one herself. She told us a red fox and pup were in the woods about a quarter of a mile away. We looked intently up the hill and saw trees and shadows. Waiting my turn, I got a peek in the scope and helped Shorty see as well.

The mother fox lazed between two trees. She glanced in the pup's direction, flattening her ears and rolling her eyes before looking away. Her offspring must have been driving her batty—I knew the look well, as I had performed the exact same eye roll as we tried to leave the cabin earlier that day. In another scope we could see the pup stomping his little feet in the dirt, creating a cloud, then running back up the small hill, having an absolute ball. With the naked eye you could see a puff of dirt in the shadows but nothing else. It was amazing to see foxes in the wild and so comfortable in their surroundings. I couldn't help but think of the bear not too far off and hoped it wasn't doubling back for a pup-cicle snack.

We ended our day by making our way up the Yellowstone River, marveling at the glory of the park. We had all been blessed with so many special memories during the week, with the bear sightings topping them all. Yellowstone will always be in my heart and we hope to go back in a few years since it's so huge with no way to see it all in one visit. Next time we will explore the southern half and maybe find Lady Luck again.

The Last Fare

John A. Brock

Where you headed?

Sure thing, buddy. That's clear on the other side of town. Good thing you called, being it's a full moon and all. I've never been superstitious but it's true what they say, a full moon brings out all the crazies. I've worked the night shift for many years, and the stories I could tell would scare even Stephen King.

You coming from the club? I don't mean to offend, but I can smell alcohol and cigarette smoke. But I know what it's like. I guess I should say I *used* to know what it's like. If the Lord allows you the years he's given me, you'll know what I'm talking about. Your mind sometimes gets stuck and you think it's forty years ago. They say time passes by so fast you don't feel it moving when you're young. But then you might be lucky enough to marry, and you see the years on your wife's face. You may be blessed with a kid or two, and they grow from a baby to a teenager in the blink of an eye. Then one day you look in the mirror and there's this old man staring back at you.

Getting older isn't much fun.

Roll down the window if you want. Heck, light up a cigarette if you feel like it. I'd join you for a smoke, but I quit years ago. Hardest habit to break. Still love the smell of cigarettes. I guess if the firsthand smoke didn't kill me, secondhand smoke might one day.

You have a girlfriend? Take it you don't since you're alone on a Saturday night. Well, technically Sunday morning now. Listen, take my advice and find yourself a sweetheart. Find one you really like and forget about the others. Sharing your life with someone is the most important thing in this world, let me tell you. When you get to be my age, you'll have someone who'll remember when you were young and could conquer the world. Someone to remember you when you were in your prime. A witness, you might say.

You don't mind me blabbing away like this, do you?

Good, because driving a taxi can be lonesome work. You pick up a group and everyone's being obnoxious, talking loud and having a good time. You feel as if you don't exist, just part of the machine taking them to their next destination. What's worse is the business person, typing away on their laptop or making deals over the phone. They hand you the fare without making eye contact, out of the cab and on their way.

Today's world, I don't know.

I'm starting to sound like a bitter old man. I guess it's good that Vince the cabbie's hanging up his hat. You, my friend, are my last passenger.

Thought I'd retire to a bungalow on a tiny island in the middle of nowhere. But the wife and I found a small house in town, something more manageable. It's hard to think about selling the house you raised your children in, but we could use the extra money. We'll have time to spend with grandkids, something I haven't had too much time for, driving this cab all night and sleeping the days away. Used to think living my last days on a tropical island would be paradise, but nothing can compare to grandchildren.

You're a good-looking kid, if you don't mind me saying. I sure wouldn't mind if someone told me the same thing! Bet you're not used to coming out of a nightclub without a little company.

You did the right thing calling for a taxi. Even a couple of beers can cloud one's driving skills. I know, unfortunately witness it every night. Lucky I haven't been involved in any major crashes, though I must've had a least a hundred near-misses through the years. Something about a red light after midnight. Either people don't care, figure there's no one else driving at that time of night, or they're too drunk to notice. They fly right through, giving you the finger if you dare honk at them.

My mother used to say nothing good happens after midnight, and for the most part, she was right. Though I'm sure some good things have happened to you after midnight!

Mind if I turn on the radio?

Thanks. I'll just turn it up just loud enough for background noise. The creaks and groans this old cab makes gets on my nerves. I'm sure the creaks and groans this cabbie makes gets on my wife's nerves, I'll tell you what!

Here's an oldie but goodie. Good old rock and roll before the Beatles changed everything. Don't get me wrong, I like the Beatles, Stones, all that sixties stuff, but they can't hold a candle to Chuck Berry or Buddy Holly, if you ask me.

This radio only picks up FM and AM, but the music I like most they don't play on FM. I have to search through the crackle of static to find the good music. The AM stations hide out like ghosts in the wavelengths, waiting for me to find them. Almost like the songs from way back are hiding, waiting to be found, and it always feels good to find one.

My father and I used to listen to the Cardinals' games. We couldn't tune into the station during the day, so if it was a day game, we were out of luck. But at night the frequency would come in loud and clear. I know St. Louis is far away, but I spent so much of my youth listening to their games I bleed Cardinal red! Maybe I can make a game up there during my newfound free time. Never seen them play in person. That may be an experience worth taking in.

My children keep trying to hook up our cars with satellite radio and our house with the internet and cable television, but I've never cared for that stuff. My grandkids make fun of my flip phone, but for me it works just fine. Maybe now I'll look into some of that technology, but for the most part seems like a waste of time. My son and daughters are always checking their phones, the kids playing their games, the screens stuck up to their eyes almost. But luckily they haven't become slaves to their phones yet. When we take them out to a dinner, we still bow our heads and silently say our thanks, and it gives me hope they're being raised right. But I guess it's only a matter of time before they feel the claws of the world clutch around them.

My kids are always texting me, and I try to reply as much as I can, but it seems ridiculous. I'd rather they call and I can hear their voice. It's so much nicer. But I grew up in a different world.

You a student? Thought so. How are you enjoying our little town? I've lived here almost my entire life. I drove a cab in Vegas for a few years, though. Didn't meet many famous people, they're more into limousines. Taking a taxi is beneath them. I did meet a lot of interesting folks, that's for sure. Far more fascinating than movie stars.

We were very young when we moved there. My wife's a nurse and was able to get a job pretty easy. This was before kids and a mortgage and all the other stuff that weighs you down. We've both wanted some new experiences before we settled down. Be sure you sow your wild oats before you start a family. They take most of your time and you tend to forget the person you were before they came along.

Like me, she worked the night shift. Didn't see much point in being married if she worked during the day and me at night, never seeing each other. That's when my internal clock shifted from being a morning person to a night owl because now I never feel awake until it's dark.

My shift started right when things were heating up on the strip. At the start, I'd pick up people from all over the world dressed up in expensive suits and fancy dresses, their shoes worth more than I'd make in a month. Everyone believed they were the ones who would slay the dragon, bring Vegas to its knees.

"Look at all these casinos," I wanted to say. "You know who pays for all of this extravagance? You do!" But I never said anything. I was part of the city and those tourists paid my salary.

The night would go by in a flash. I'd deliver a fare to a casino where another fare would be waiting. Up and down the street all night long. It was like a maniacal merry-go-round, driving by the same light shows and hearing the passengers awe and ooh like rubes.

When the sun came up, you'd pick up some of the same folks but their demeanor had changed. Some of them looked devastated. Driving along in silence, you wondered how much money they lost or what bad choices were haunting them. You could worry about those type of things, how they might have messed up their lives or scarred their souls, but I learned my job was to drive and all other thoughts wouldn't do either of us any good.

One of my regular passengers was a stripper. In the morning I'd pick her up in front of her club and she'd have a cup of coffee for me. I've always remembered that little act of kindness. That first time she stepped into my cab, I made the mistake of judging her, but as we talked I realized she was only doing what she needed to do to survive. Her abusive husband skipped town when she told him she was pregnant, and she stripped to pay for raising her son and rent. The basics. It's sad, but sometimes you have to do what you have to do just to exist. Doesn't say too much about this world, does it?

Linda was her name, and she talked a lot about her life before moving to Vegas. Some of the most heartbreaking stuff you ever heard. No father. All types of abuse by a steady string of her mother's boyfriends. Then she gets married and her husband slaps her around. Make a Lifetime movie look like a Hallmark movie. But when I asked her about her work, she surprised me. She said she loved being on stage because no man was allowed to touch her. If anyone tried, a bodyguard would be there in a flash and give the creep a couple of shots to the face before dragging him out the door. For her, the job gave her all she needed: money, shelter, admiration.

One time my wife and I are at the zoo, and who did I happen to see but Linda and her young son. They were watching the monkeys and her son was staring wide-eyed at them swinging around. I'd never seen Linda smile before, but as she watched her son, her face was filled with bliss and contentment.

And this may seem a bit dramatic, but at that moment I decided we had to get out of that place. I knew someday I wanted to start a family, and I wanted to raise them in a more quiet part of the world. A few weeks later we packed up our stuff and drove back home. Been here ever since.

Looks like we're almost there. I can't believe how this town has grown. Several years ago this was the edge of town and now it's filled with houses and apartment complexes. Our house used to be in a pretty good neighborhood, but it's gone downhill the last few years. Someone moved the tracks and now we're on the wrong side.

I shouldn't say that. Some wonderful families have moved in. Every Saturday's there's always some type of celebration going on at someone's house on the street. My wife hates the noise and traffic but I don't mind. It's nice to see families enjoying each other's company, still loving life.

Don't get me wrong, I still love life. But the world can drag you down. Time moves so fast sometimes I forget what season it is. One week it's summer, the next winter. They all blur together. And then on top of that your body starts to break down and it's an effort just to climb out of bed. Maybe that's all death is, the absence of time.

I think about death sometimes. Get to be my age, you can't help it. But the strange thing was I worried about it more when I was younger. Back then, I didn't a clue what my legacy would be, but now

I can see how I lived my life with all the blessings and tragedies, and can be at total peace realizing I lived the best life I could.

When I was younger, I'd wonder how I'd kick the bucket. Old or young? Would it be painful? How many friends and family would attend my funeral? Pretty selfish of me. But now, I think of others. My wife is as beautiful as she's ever been, and just when I think I can't love her more, she'll do some small thing that makes me love her a little more. I hope I go first. I don't want to see someone precious as her fade away.

Here we are. No, you don't owe me anything. I should be paying you for listening to my nonsense this entire ride. Besides, you're my last fare and it just seems right.

Take care, and I hope some of my ramblings serve you well.

No, keep your money in your pocket.

Are you sure? Well, thanks for the tip!

May the stars always shine on you, my friend!

The Watch Repair

Karen Gammage

The young strawberry blond nursing student, Marie, was outgoing and enthusiastic. She enjoyed every part of nursing and looked forward to every new experience no matter how much work it involved. Each nursing school is different as to how much clinical experience is a part of the training along with the classroom training. Marie appreciated that her school had more bedside training because she knew she would learn more by actually seeing what she had only read about.

It was now time for Marie to go through her Psychiatric rotation. She was rather nervous about this training. Patients were mostly presented as blank looking, zoned out like zombies, or as talking gibberish. But she'd heard the horror stories of wild patients, had seen the movies where patients became violent.

Marie decided to try and keep a clear head and not let her imagination get the better of her. She told herself that she would be talking with people with all kinds of problems, most brought on by extremely stressful situations and poor problem solving, or poor decision making and the consequences that evolved. Of course, some mental illnesses are caused by chemical imbalances. That's what the books said anyway. She was at least relieved that, as a student, she wouldn't be put in with the criminally insane. But then, what would she actually see? Tomorrow was her first day.

At 6:30 the next morning, Marie reached the outer doors of the Psychiatric unit. The students stood ready to proceed into the unit for report. Every day the students went to a unit to work, the day was to begin with report. The big difference with this unit was that the doors were locked, and they had to wait to go in as a group accompanied by their instructor. They waited until all of the students had gathered before the instructor pushed the buzzer that alerted the nurse's station. The instructor identified herself and announced their expected arrival. In a couple of minutes the Department Director arrived at the door to allow them to proceed into the unit. The Director introduced herself and stated that they were happy to have the students come. She asked if any of the students had been on a psychiatric unit before. All ten students were noticeably wide eyed and apprehensive as they shook their heads.

The Director led them down the hall to a staff area, past patients in the hallway. Some stood talking with each other, others sat on chairs or even on the floor. Some teens were standing around a pool table in the wide hallway socializing. The patients seemed as curious about the nursing students as the students were about the patients. The students stood out like a sore thumb as they marched past in a group wearing student uniforms while patients and staff wore regular street attire. The only difference was that the staff wore name tags.

When the student group reached the staff room, the Director stated that for the first day they would become acquainted with the unit. She gave them special instructions of etiquette for the unit before they had patient contact. They were not expected to give therapy to patients. She explained that a lot of the daily care simply involved conversation with the patients along with making sure the patients were able to care for themselves. Some patients were so mentally disconnected from reality by stress that they stopped normal daily functions including dressing or eating. Nurses helped them with the simplest of functions before the patients could be helped mentally with coping skills. Patients were encouraged to participate in therapy sessions and were expected to dress and attend meals with the group for socialization. Most were in some degree of progress. These patients were not hostile, but some were in a state of confusion or depression. Students would be acquainting themselves with patients as a part of the socialization process but weren't allowed to sit in on therapy sessions due to privacy issues since they were not regular staff.

There were some basic rules that everyone was expected to follow on the unit:

- Students were not allowed to unlock the door without a staff member present.

- Don't allow yourself to be caught behind a closed door alone with a patient. The Director stated that though a patient could seem quite calm and in a normal state on the outside, that was not necessarily what was going on on the inside. Some could be quite devious.

- Be smart; don't turn your back on a patient, especially if they appear at all irritated.

- Never let patients have cigarettes if they are out of the smoking area and don't leave them alone when they are smoking. Make sure that cigarettes are completely extinguished before leaving the area.

- Don't carry letters or messages off the unit for patients or run errands for them. The patients have routines and systems to follow for messaging and visitation. It keeps drugs from being passed to them from friends or family.

- Don't keep secrets for patients. If they ask you to keep a secret, tell them that what they may tell might help them to progress and it has to be reported when it is not known for their own good. Be honest and up front.

- Document both good attitudes and appropriate reactions and handling of situations as well as poor attitudes or acting out kinds of behavior. It helps to reveal progress and plan appropriate treatment.

It was soon time to progress to the patient areas. The students tried to spread out and not bunch together even though they were unsure of themselves. The students started out together to group areas to visit with patients. Marie noted that one end of the floor was an adult area and the other end of the floor was a teenage end. There was a game room, patient rooms, a smoking area, and a central nurse's area. There was also a large room for group therapy and an exercise area. Marie began to observe all of the types of patients to try to distinguish diagnoses. The students would have to eventually pick a patient and write a paper about their individual contact with that patient and do a patient study on their diagnosis. It was somewhat easy to pick out some of the types even though it was the first day.

Marie started into the smoking area where a small group of patients were visiting. She felt it would be a good place to start observing. Some of the patients were talkative and wanted to know who the strange nurses were and why they were there. A person that was off to one side became very quiet and distant and withdrew from any conversation. He offered little or no comments with the nurses even when they tried to bring him into the conversation. One lady was in a manic stage of bipolar disease. She was in continuous motion. She was overdressed in several layers of clothing which were unnecessary and didn't go together. The layers included a dress as well as pants. She wore a slip over the dress and then a skirt. Her makeup was also over applied with bright red rouge on cheeks, blobbed-on uneven eye makeup, and lipstick that did not stay within the lip lines.

Marie noted that the woman wore what appeared to be every piece of jewelry she owned. She must have had on ten necklaces, two different pairs of earrings, two or more rings on every finger, and several bracelets. She had a flip pack of matches she had received from one of the nurses so that she could light a cigarette. She would light one cigarette and take a few puffs and then light another while the first one still lay in the ashtray lit.

As she moved continuously, she began to talk to no one in particular while lighting and flipping matches one after the other. She would light a match, fascinated with the flame for a few seconds, and then flip the match, sometimes at the ashtray and sometimes at people sitting in the lounge. She launched one into the lap of Marie who was wearing a skirt-type uniform. Marie was sitting in an lounge chair and the woman, a tall big-boned person, stood in front of Marie, trapping her in the chair. It was impossible for Marie to get up or move away. Marie swept the match out of her skirt fold as quickly as she could. One of the other students quickly tapped the woman on the shoulder and asked her a question. The woman turned around. Marie scurried out of the chair and was much relieved to be able to distance herself. One of the regular staff retrieved the matches from the patient, reminding her that the matches were only for lighting cigarettes.

Feeling a need to change scenery, Marie decided to move away from the lounge and went to the game area to observe and talk to a few of the teens. The teens ranged from very depressed and introverted to the opposite pole—talkative, sassy and belligerent. Marie moved from place to place, observing all types of patients and talking to a few patients she would consider for the paper she had to write.

It was finally time for lunch. The students went to the same dining area as the patients and sat down among them. Nurses would watch eating habits and observe for incidents of choking as some patients were on medications that caused sedation. On occasion, staff also needed to manage patient behavior that might lead to food fights at the community tables. Sitting with patients created a family-type atmosphere and sometimes made it easier to draw patients into conversation.

While sitting at the table, Marie noted that her watch had stopped working. She pecked at it with her finger to see if it would restart. When that didn't help, she removed it, held the watch straps in her right hand, and tapped tit again with her left index finger. When this failed, she popped the watch against the palm of her hand. A polite blond-headed patient sitting across from her, who had been introduced to her as Daniel, asked what was wrong. Marie stated, "I've been having some problems off and on with my watch and now its stopped. I'm trying to see if I can get it going."

"Here, let me have it." Daniel held out his hand. "I'm pretty good at fixing watches. Maybe I can help."

Marie handed him her watch and took another bite of her lunch. He took the watch and inspected the casing and the hands of the watch. He tried to adjust the pin to set the watch and see if it would stimulate the watch to work. The minute hand didn't go into motion. He removed the back of the watch casing as everyone at the table looked on while he diligently went to work. Daniel emptied the watch from its casing and laid the inside workings on the dining table. He laid the casing and the watch band out on the table to the side. He reached down and removed his shoe and brought it up as if inspecting for a pebble inside. Then he took hold of the toe of the shoe and began to hammer the watch with the heel. Springs, dials, and the workings of the watch went in every direction. Everyone looked on with mouths open wide in disbelief at what they were observing. It had happened so quickly and without notice.

Daniel quickly and quietly gathered the pieces of the watch, scooping them ever so carefully and attentively into his hand to make sure that he had gathered every tiny spring and screw. He handed all of the pieces over to Marie and said with a smile of earnest contentment in his accomplishment, "There you are. All fixed." There was nothing Marie could do except say, "Thank you." She had willingly handed over the watch without thinking of anything other than a positive outcome.

Daniel excused himself from the table and Marie placed the demolished pieces in her uniform pocket. She learned a valuable lesson and had a souvenir to remind her of her first day.

Shoes

Crystal Phares

I met a man, and he broke my heart.

No, not like you're thinking. This isn't a story about unrequited love, or an affair gone wrong.

I deal with hundreds of people a day. Most flow in and out of my world with barely a ripple. Some are special and stay with me longer, like Mr. Jim and his shoes.

When he came in and asked to use the facilities, I pointed across the lobby and went back to answering the phone and responding to emails. Mondays are busy, and I forgot about Mr. Jim until I looked up to see him standing a few feet from my desk.

He waited for me to finish another endless, pointless phone call and gestured at himself and then to me, asking if he could come closer. I put on my best professional smile—you know the one—bright, shiny, and empty as a lightbulb, and beckoned him over. I'm sad to say, that was the first time I looked at him. Really looked at him, not *through* him.

I'd love to excuse myself and say I was just busy. Yes, the phones rang, emails were coming in faster than I could respond, but that isn't the only reason I didn't take the time to see him. Honestly, I was on autopilot. Yes, I was working, but in the back of my mind I thought about what to make my husband and three kids for dinner, had anyone bothered to clean up the mess from breakfast, or had they just made more messes for me to clean up when I got home? At only 10 in the morning, I was already exhausted thinking about everything I needed to do when I got home. I was *too busy* to be bothered by anyone else who needed something.

I was being a terrible human being and wanted to be left alone. But then I looked at Mr. Jim. In his mid-60's and balding on top, his curly black hair reached his shoulders in the back. His suit was nice but well worn, and tailored to a man smaller than him. The front gaped between the buttons, and the pants were inches too short. His shirt, a shade somewhere between pink and tan, had a ragged collar from being pressed too many times. His mismatched socks showed plainly under the hem of his trousers, one navy blue, the other pale gray.

His shoes . . . well, his shoes caught my attention. The black dress shoes he wore were polished to a mirror shine without a single scuff mark.

Thanking me for my time, he shook my hand and introduced himself as Jim. He told me how hard it was to find polite people anymore and he knew I'd been raised right because I smiled and said all the right things. I didn't feel proud at that moment. I knew if my mother had heard the thoughts in my head she would have had a few words to say to me. Because she had raised me right. She raised me to be friendly and charitable, and to always, *always*, pay attention to people. "Everyone is fighting their own battle," she'd tell me. "Give them the respect they deserve for fighting another day."

In my head, I apologized to both my mother and the man in front of me. He'd obviously taken the time to clean himself up in the restroom. His hair was a bit damp, and his bushy beard, too, but his face was clean, and his deep brown eyes sparkled. We talked about how hot it was for only being May and how pretty the new park down the street was. He picked up the framed photos and the sparkle disappeared from his eyes, heartache replacing the joy from a moment before. He commented on the photo of my kids, telling me how lucky I am to have three healthy, happy babies. I agreed and we talked about my kids for a few minutes. I asked if he had any children. He didn't answer, but his silence told its own story. A few more minutes of idle chit chat, where I ignored my ringing phone and the string of emails popping up, and then he was gone. Walking out the door and out of my life.

I wondered where Mr. Jim called home, if he had a home. I imagined him sitting in a smoke filled bar, because the scent of whiskey laced his breath. I speculated on a family long gone and a loneliness that haunted his soul. The sadness in his eyes told me a story he didn't want to share.

When I got in bed that night his image troubled me and I described him to my drowsy husband. When I told him about Jim's shoes, he stopped me.

He must have been military. The words rumbled out in rough sleepiness. My mind filled with images of Mr. Jim. A young man polishing his boots, putting on a uniform and fighting for what he believed in, no matter how terrified he was, no matter how much he missed his family. Seconds later, the movie in my head showed him coming home to a wife and small children who couldn't understand where daddy had been and why he had nightmares. The wife couldn't comprehend horrors he refused to share with her.

I imagined long nights of worry where he disappeared from their bed after waking from another night terror, the smell of cheap whiskey on his breath when he finally came back. In my mind I saw her pack the kids in the car, look at him one last time, and drive away. Knowing she had lost the man that she loved. Realizing that man never came home from the war.

My eyes filled as another image played across the movie screen of my mind. I saw his tears and his endless shoe polishing as he drank away the rest of his life.

I worried about Mr. Jim. Every day for two weeks, I left for work early, driving endless blocks around my office looking for him. I hugged my family a little tighter and a little longer as soon as I got home. I listened to made up stories, made cookies with my kids even though exhaustion weighed on me. I played one more game of Go Fish before bed, and made love to my husband with more passion.

I never did find Mr. Jim.

Until I saw a photo of a young, handsome soldier next to a short obituary. I left work hours early and sat in the back of a quiet church that smelled of candle wax and furniture polish. After the service, I shook the hands of Mr. Jim's two sons, who had eyes just like Mr. Jim, and knelt down to eye level with his five-year-old granddaughter. I took their small family to lunch and told them the story of Mr. Jim changing my life. Ella, Mr. Jim's granddaughter, hugged me before she left and thanked me for telling her a story about a man she'd never meet.

I'll always be thankful to Mr. Jim and his spotless shoes. In only a few minutes this stranger brought me back into focus and reminded me of the important things in life. He reminded me to *look* at people, really listen to what they were saying, and to give with my whole heart, even when it is breaking.

Crystal Phares lives in Amarillo, Texas with her super supportive husband of seventeen years, three amazing children, two lazy boxers, and a grumpy hedgehog. By day, Crystal is a museum curator, writing exhibit texts, cleaning artifacts, designing entertaining exhibits, and doing research. After work she spends time laughing with her family, supporting causes that are close to her heart, reading everything she can get her hands on, writing short stories, working on a novel, and drinking as much coffee as is humanly possible.

Shackled Behind the Piano

Suzana Sandoval

My perch was a lonely place. I was chained to it, the shackles invisible—shackles of ignorance and fear.

I remember my first day of school; a day I had looked forward to all summer. I was a big girl now. I had conjured up what it would be like and the day was finally here.

I couldn't contain my excitement as we walked into the enormous building that housed classrooms first through eighth grade. I danced around Grandma, then bounded up the steps of the school house as I called after: "Hurry, Abuelita, hurry."

Upon entering the cool cavernous building, I drank in the comforting aromas: waxy crayons, paper, and pencil shavings.

The bell shrilled.

"Where do I go, Grandma?"

She pointed to the end of the hall, "Over there, the last door with the rainbow on it. See it?" Taking me by the hand she walked me to the room. At the door she gently prodded me, "Now go." Timidity held me fast. Uncertain on how to enter the classroom, I looked around for Grandma but her bent form had scurried out the heavy double doors that slammed fierce and final. With hands clasped behind my back and in a show of respect, I lowered my eyes.

"Ah, Susana there you are," Mrs. Q, the first-grade teacher, quipped. "Come in. Take a seat." I remained immobile. "Come! Come!" She pulled out a chair.

Children sat at long tables. I didn't look like them. Amid sneers and giggles, I walked across the room to the chair Mrs. Q indicated. Giving my classmates a side glance, I saw their eyes locked on the hem of my dress. Well above knobby knees, it made my legs appear wonky like a foal. A slow hot tint crawled up my neck.

My brown high top shoes caused the most commotion. The night before, Grandpa gave the shoe laces a vigorous scrubbing. He cleaned and polished the decrepit shoes, but all the Shinola shoe polish in the world couldn't hide the creases and scuff marks. Tears stung my eyes at the sight of the lacy white socks and black Patten shoes the girls wore.

Jostling each other, the boys poked their heads under the table to take another look at my shoes while the girls whispered in each other's ears and tittered. I tossed my long black braids interwoven with red ribbons behind my back, wishing I could disappear.

Time crawled. By days-end, the excitement of school had vanished. At home, I recounted my harrowing experience to Grandma. "I won't be going back to school, Abuelita," I lamented.

Grandma didn't look up from the tortilla she was rolling out. "It's not our choice. You must go to school." Unperturbed, she continued working the doughy disc.

"I don't look like them, Grandma."

"I know Honey, but it's important that you always look like yourself."

Silent tears rolled down my face. I ran out the door and behind the house to cry.

The following day, I returned to school with my homework undone. My grandmother, being a Spanish speaker, couldn't help me. Together we looked at the pictures in the primary book. It didn't take long to go from cover to cover drawing the conclusion that the characters were a family that had two pets—a dog and a cat.

After a couple of days of struggling with the English language, unable to follow directions or do my homework, Mrs. Q labeled me unteachable. To keep me from distracting the class, she gave me a seat on a high stool behind the piano. The class erupted into bedlam as she led me to a place of disgrace. My soul broke.

By giving me a seat behind the piano, Mrs. Q. made my life more difficult. Her actions gave the students unspoken permission to ridicule me more than ever.

"Hey dunce." Napoleon, the boy with rust-colored hair and an odd haircut, taunted me during recess. He had a smattering of dark freckles across his nose and over both cheeks. The freckles reminded me of fly poop. Hey poop face, I thought.

"I don't want to go to school Grandma," I bemoaned each morning. "The girls laugh at me and the boys pull my braids." Hot, salty tears poured down my face, clinging for dear life to my chin before dropping off. "Please Grandma, I want to stay home with you."

She pulled a tissue and compassionately wiped my nose. With a warm, wet wash cloth, she cleaned my face.

"Honey, things change. Nothing stays the same. All of this will pass." She brushed my hair gently. "You go to school because you must. You'll find that in life, we often do what we have to do and not what we want." She planted a dry but encouraging kiss on my head.

"Struggle is an advantage, my child. I know it's a hard for you to believe, but that is what builds inner strength. There will be many days when you'll need to draw from it." Her sedating touch assuaged my sorrow. "You'll see someday, adversity is a blessing turned inside out." She braided a yellow ribbon into my hair. I gave what she said a good bit of thought. I didn't understand, but I believed her.

My blessing came that day at recess, or at least it seemed like a blessing to me.

Napoleon circled me like a vulture. I stood on the steps of the massive building with my back to him. I watched his reflection in the vertical glass pane of the door. As he sprinted forward, I moved up one step. With failing arms, he grabbed at the emptiness and went down on his knees. My heart rejoiced.

"Look at Napoleon." Albert, Napoleon's best friend, pointed and bent over in gut-busting laughter. "A girl beat him up."

Hooting and hollering, the rest of his buddies chimed in. Napoleon turned scarlet. He instantly got to his feet. With clenched fists, Napoleon shot straight for the cluster of boys. They scattered like billiard balls with Napoleon is hot pursuit.

The girls sitting in a circle playing jacks stopped to watch the commotion. They seemed to be as delighted as I was that Napoleon got the short end of the stick.

"He looked so funny when Suzana moved and he went down on his knees," Amy Reynolds laughed. Billie Jean remarked, "Yea, his face turned red like a tomato."

"Suzana, "Amy demanded, "Come play jacks with us." The girls scooted around making room for me.

I found my oasis in recess. It gave me a break from the misery behind the piano. Amy would become my best friend.

Day after lonely day, I sat perched on the stool behind the piano. Unable to participate with the class, I grew weary. Sometimes I nodded off, noisily catching myself before I hit the floor. A vigorous uproar followed. Mrs. Q tapped her yardstick on the floor, "Enough, children!" Looking over her glasses she chastised, "Pay attention, Susana, and sit up straight." I cringed.

She didn't know I had figured out all the characters in the *Dick and Jane* book. Spot and Puff saved my sanity

"Grandma, I want a white and black dog. I'll call him Spot like in my book" She didn't look up from her mending. Her demeanor remained unfazed and frozen like an ancient statue. Grandma's habitually delayed response irked me. Her deft fingers created delicate stitches and without looking up she grimaced.

"Espot?" Again she grimaced. "What kind of a name is Espot?"

"It's what the people in my book call their pets. I like the name Grandma!"

"You have Pancho. One dog is enough." I didn't give up. "But Pancho is brown, dirty and ugly like my shoes.

"Silly girl, you've not yet learned what is important."

"What is important?"

"You will see." Grand snipped the extra thread. She looked up. "You will see."

My English vocabulary increased and by Spring I had earned the honor of sitting among my peers. When Mrs. Q made the announcement, everyone clapped. I was overjoyed that Mrs. Q assigned me a seat next to Amy.

The lesson I learned behind the piano that excited me most didn't come from a book. I learned that education is freedom. Education released me from my shackles.

www.ingramcontent.com/pod-product-compliance
Lightning Source LLC
Chambersburg PA
CBHW032146170626
46808CB00006B/2382